The Catholic Cowboy Way

Fr. Bryce Lungren

The Catholic Cowboy Way

Finding Peace and Purpose
on the Bronc Called Life

SOPHIA INSTITUTE PRESS
Manchester, New Hampshire

Sophia Institute Press
Box 5284, Manchester, NH 03108
1-800-888-9344

www.SophiaInstitute.com

Sophia Institute Press® is a registered trademark of Sophia Institute.

paperback ISBN 978-1-64413-806-9

ebook ISBN 978-1-64413-807-6

Library of Congress Control Number: 2022947778

First printing

*To all the men and women in my life whose good example
has helped form me into the man I am today,
but especially to Mom and Dad, whose steadfast love
has taught me what it means to be a son.*

Contents

The Catholic Cowboy Way

Introduction

It was a hot, dusty July night at the Campbell County fairgrounds. The stands were light, but the chutes were full. As I got a seat on this big buckskin, I pulled my hat down low, said a prayer, and nodded my head. The gateman cracked the latch, and the announcer yelled, "Fr. Bryce!"

Man, this horse could buck! But what surprised me the most was that I was still in the saddle to recognize it. That was short-lived, though. By the fourth buck, I was off to the side and eventually in the dirt. Two things came to my mind in that moment: first, that my shoulder hurt and, second, that I should've listened to my old man.

See, this wasn't my first rodeo. But it wasn't far from it. In the face of the 2020 fear pandemic, I decided to try my hand at saddle bronc. Why? I guess it was just on my heart. By the time I hit the Campbell County Ranch Rodeo, I was two broncs deep. But those were straight-up saddle bronc rides, where a cowboy holds the hack rein with only one hand and squeezes the swells in the saddle with his thighs. After those two quick dismounts, I decided to try ranch bronc.

In ranch bronc, you use your regular saddle with a night latch of sorts to grab on to as if ole Chief just blew up as you were riding across the prairie. Well, being a rookie, I also jacked my stirrups up real high so I could use my swells too. I was looking for all the help I could get.

Dad called me early that morning and said, "Son, I think you should lengthen your stirrups." "Dad," I said, "I've got a game plan." Well, my plan failed. My feet were out of the stirrups before that horse cleared the gate. It was just a matter of time before the rest of me was out of the saddle too. The moral of the story: listen to Dad!

Sound familiar? It's an age-old problem. In fact, our first parents invented the scenario. Through them, we have inherited the tendency to rebel against our fathers. This usually manifests itself first with our own dads. What's the saying? *When I was eighteen, my dad didn't know anything. When I turned twenty-one, I was surprised how much he learned in three years.*

Life is an analogy of our relationship with God. Just as we have the tendency not to listen to our earthly fathers, so do we also have the tendency not to listen to our heavenly Father.

I don't know about you, but over the years, I have come to learn that the Father truly knows best. And why wouldn't He? He created us. Not only did He make us, but He created us to be happy and to fulfill a mission.

That indeed is good news. However, what we think will make us happy and what will actually make us happy may be two different things. What we think our mission in life is and what we are actually designed for may not be the same.

People often ask me when I knew I wanted to be a priest. I reply that I never wanted to be a priest and I still don't. But God created me for this, and I am happier and more fulfilled in this way of life than I would have been in any other that I could have ever imagined. But I have to daily trust that Dad knows best. Left solely to my own passions, my life would be a trainwreck. But when I listen to the Father and trust that He has my best interests in mind, I'm the happiest man alive.

So how do we get there? Jesus. *Jesus is the way, the truth, and the life. No one comes to the Father except through Him.*[1] He is our big Brother, who has plowed the way home. He teaches us by example how to handle life. He guides us by the wisdom of His Catholic Church. And most of all, He continues to lead us by the voice of His Spirit dwelling in our hearts. I have no problem saying that Jesus is a cowboy. He's brave. He's bold. But most of all, He's a Son.

Cowboys aren't born. They're discovered. There is a cowboy in all of us. There's a brave spirit. There's a bold determination. And most of all, there's a beloved son of God the Father. This is the Catholic Cowboy Way. If left to ourselves, life will buck us off. If we're tuned in to the Father through the Holy Spirit dwelling in our hearts, then life is fun, and we get the job done.

[1] John 14:6.

My Heroes Have Always Been Cowboys

Growing up, my happiest memories were always of brandings. Each year over the Fourth of July, we would drive up to my grandpa's land in the Big Horn Mountains of Wyoming and work cattle for a few days. There, along with much family and friends, we would separate the cows and brand the calves.

I say *we*, but I was mostly a spectator at these events because they only lasted in this venue until I was about five. Though I was young, these original rodeos set the course for the rest of my life.

Watching through the weathered corral poles, I witnessed men and women, boys and girls, giving all they had to get a job done. I saw my dad rope and drag calves to the fire. I saw my granddad put his boot on the hip of a calf while branding it with the *lazy 6 over 6*. I saw my uncles wrestle calves to the ground as if they were scared of nothing, and my brothers and cousins trying to do the same. And after all that, I saw Grandma and Mom and my aunts providing a feast for us back at the cabin.

These were my heroes growing up, and they still are, it seems. They were my role models, men and women whom I aspired to be like. Their witness and example spoke volumes to me.

Later in life, when we buried my grandpa, I recalled four things that he verbally taught me. He would say, *Never cut your fingernails too short. Only back up as far as you need to. Always wear a hat.* And, *Never quit driving.* Those four things that Grandpa said to me stick in my mind. But the example of his life was an endless school of virtue that motivated me to be the best man I can be.

We lead by example, and we learn by example. When I graduated from high school, I moved to Montana to work for my uncle. He was a man I admired. He worked hard and practiced his Catholic Faith. And through his example, he taught me to do the same.

I knew he influenced me, but I didn't know to what degree until I went back home that fall and it was pointed out that I had taken on his mannerisms. Without knowing it, I had started to talk the way he talked and walk the way he walked, which, in this case, was a good thing. He was a good role model and helped me make good decisions in my life just by the example of his life.

Other people rub off on us. Almost through osmosis, we become like those we run with, for good or ill. I think of St. Paul, who stated, "Bad company ruins good morals."[2] Or St. Teresa of Ávila, who is to have said, "Show me your friends, and I'll show you yourself."

We are forever impressionable people. And I am convinced that no matter how old we are, we never stop having role models. Whether we know it or not, we all have our heroes who continually shape who we are becoming.

My life made a distinctive shift when Jesus started to become my main role model. I am forever thankful that when I left home, I never stopped going to Mass. Through those intimate encounters

---

[2]   1 Corinthians 15:33.

with our Lord, I slowly began to *put on the mind of Christ*.[3] Listening to His voice, during and outside of Mass, I found myself starting to talk like Him. Learning from the example of His life, which the Gospel authors penned, I also found myself beginning to walk like Him.

What I found fun about getting to know Jesus is that He is a real person, and not simply a character in a book. The Gospels paint a partial picture of the Man's life, which is undoubtedly important, but I love reading between the lines, filling in the gaps.

Take the *hidden years*, the years of Jesus between twelve and thirty. A lot must have happened, but none of it is written down. As a young man learning about the Man, I also began to ponder what His life would have been like at my age.

This is not simple abstract speculation. Jesus reveals Himself to us when we do this. Not that my envisioning of His early years is objectively infallible, but it is subjectively personal. I began to *relate* to Him, as one man does to another.

Later in life, I had the opportunity to visit the Holy Land and see Jesus' hometown of Nazareth. This *spiritual relating* truly hit home in that moment when I gazed from His front porch across the valley to Mount Tabor. In the Gospels, St. Luke tells us the story of when Jesus and His boys, Peter, James, and John, hiked up Mount Tabor and He was *transfigured* before them. In that revelation, the Father spoke to them and said, *This is my beloved son with whom I am well pleased. Listen to Him!*[4]

I always loved this story, but what I realized on that day is that this was probably not a new event for our Lord. I could just imagine Him getting off work at five o'clock on a Friday and heading for

---

[3] 1 Corinthians 2:16.
[4] Luke 9:35.

the hills, as we all do. He probably spent that time retreating from the craziness of first-century Israel and just chilled with His Father. I'm sure, too, that if Coors Light were around back then, He would have had a few with Him as well. The prayer encounter that the boys later witnessed was probably something Jesus experienced regularly as He spent these weekends in the woods.

The point here is that Jesus relates to us in our personal lives and situations. I was a workingman, and so was He. And in this pondering of His life, I came to know not simply a historical figure but a Man who spoke to me personally.

There is so much depth to relating to Jesus in this way. On paper, my life might look extraordinary. But in real life, it is *extraordinarily ordinary* at best. What I mean by this is that all our lives have the opportunity to be *extraordinary* in the light of Jesus the Redeemer.

Once I really got to know Him, I started to backtrack through my past experiences. Believe me, not all of them rest on a bed of roses. But walking through my memories with Jesus I was able to *glean the good* out of them.

All the sudden, my life story became refined. Even my bad choices were turned into *good* fruit. The thing is, my life growing up was normal and, most of the time, was even boring. But so was Jesus'.

His hometown, like mine, was average. In Him there was no *stately bearing*,[5] nor was there in me. He was a simple laborer, and so was I. That's what is so marvelous about relating ourselves to Jesus. He brings out the *good* in us. He makes the ordinary extraordinary. And He turns evil into good.

What is also beautiful in this way of spiritual relating to Jesus is that I could also trace back to Him the things that I admired

---

[5]   Isaiah 53:2.

in my childhood heroes. Jesus was hardworking. He wasn't scared of anything. He was all about getting the job done, and He knew how to have fun. The cowboy spirit has its roots in Jesus Christ.

What are the characteristics that make Jesus and the cowboy so universally admired? I can wear my Roman collar anywhere in the world and people would recognize it. I can also wear my cowboy hat anywhere in the world and people would recognize it. The common ground between Jesus and the cowboy is what I call *childlike seriousness*.

Childlike seriousness is the disposition of having fun and getting the job done. Let's take the iconic cowboy. He is a man who is humble, not in a hurry, and has a broad perspective of life, always looking toward a brighter day. He usually rides for another man's brand, travels light, and is willing to sacrifice himself to accomplish whatever task is at hand. Yet he does it with a light heart. There may be hay to put up or cattle to calve, but when the opportunity to go fishing arises, he's gone with the wind and doesn't look back.

This isn't irresponsible. It's just knowing that he is a part of something much bigger than himself. Even when the workload is daunting, he can still have a cheerful spirit, knowing that God has provided before and He will provide again.

In a sense, the weight of the world doesn't rest on his shoulders. Maybe this comes from his connection with nature or from having much time in solitude to ponder the deeper meanings in life. Wherever it comes from, the cowboy carries a childlike seriousness within him.

Jesus has much of the same disposition. He knows He's on a mission. In fact, much of the literature we have about Him suggests that *accomplishing His father's will*[6] was His sole purpose in life.

---

[6]   John 6:38.

The Gospels depict a man who is so driven to die that nothing could stop Him. But He also had a broad—an eternal—perspective in life. He saw through the sacrifice on the Cross to the glory of the Resurrection to come.[7] He, too, was humble. Being God incarnate, He never flaunted or abused His power. He always used it for the common good and not for self-aggrandizement.[8]

What I love most about the Man I call Lord is that that He was childlike. He knew that before He was the Messiah, He was first of all the Son of God. He called God *Abba*[9] with the tenderness of a child calling out for his *daddy*. He carried Himself through life with the confidence that comes only from the conviction that God will provide in all circumstances. He took time in the mountains to recreate with His Father.[10] And He spent time with His friends Martha, Mary, and Lazarus.[11]

But what makes Jesus infinitely superior to us is that even though He had the interior freedom that the world didn't depend on Him, it in fact did. That's why we have so much to learn from our Lord. He carried His Cross well and can teach us how to do the same.

He is the *prototypical* Man. All things good in mankind can be traced back to Him; *all were created through him; all were created for him*.[12] Jesus invented childlike seriousness, and if we follow Him, we can learn the same.

This Catholic Cowboy Way of relating to Jesus is not just for those on horseback. It's a discipline and disposition that all of us can tap into. But the only way to get there is to get *raw and real*.

---

[7] See Hebrews 12:2
[8] See Philippians 2:6–11.
[9] Mark 14:36.
[10] See Matthew 14:23.
[11] John 12:1–3.
[12] Colossians 1:16.

In other words, to encounter Jesus in a personal way, we have to get off the surface of life and into our hearts. We have to be honest with ourselves in order to be honest with God. We have to acknowledge the good, the bad, and the ugly within our own lives in order to encounter the God-Man who is the source of all that is good; who took on all that is bad in order to redeem it; and who came to help us persevere through all that is ugly.

I remember in seminary the buzzword was *vulnerability*. *Just be vulnerable, man.* I get it, be open. Be in touch with your thoughts, feelings, and desires.

But there is something lacking in the masculine department with this phrase. If I'm trotting across the pasture next to my buddy Zeke and I tell him to open up and *be vulnerable,* I might get a string of beechnut in my lap. But if I simply say, "Be raw and real, bro," then we might just get somewhere. And it'll likely be a lot more colorful than his getting in touch with his feminine side.

Don't get me wrong. I'm forever thankful for my seminary formation and how it helped me stay in touch with my heart. But for your average Joe, *vulnerability* is not in our vocabulary. *Raw and real* is, though.

Cowboys already live by this. Most tell it like it is. And most, like Jesus, can smell inauthenticity a mile away. The trick is to take this brutal honesty and use it in our relationship with God. Jesus is raw and real. Look at Him hanging on the Cross. No duplicity there. His entire being is there for the world to see.

Being raw and real does not mean that we hang our dirty laundry out for everyone to see. But it does mean that if we want to encounter Jesus, we need to meet Him where He's at.

Jesus is so multifaceted. In one instance, He's our wounded Healer, ready to heal our injuries incurred by our sins and the sins of others. In another moment, He's our Brother, coaching us on how to live life and fulfill the Father's will. In the next, He's our Savior, leading us across death and into eternal life. But in order to continually encounter Jesus' raw-and-realness, we need to follow His path.

This is not always the easiest enterprise, but it's not the most complicated either. If being raw and real is the dirt road to encountering Jesus, then the vehicle to travel down it is *faith*.

It takes *faith* because with it comes the assurance that I won't get burned. If we believe that Jesus is who He says He is, God, Savior, Healer, and so forth, then we can have the confidence to go to the depths of our being with Him.

We see it all the time in the Gospels: men and women risking their reputations to encounter Jesus. Think of the woman with a bleeding hemorrhage who came up behind Him and, after touching His cloak, was healed. *Go in peace, your faith has made you well,* He said.[13]

Or the numerous blind men who pleaded with Him to see again. *Do you believe I can heal you?* Jesus would ask them. *Then let it be done according to your faith,* He'd say.[14] Imagine the courage it took for them to step out of the crowd and call on Jesus. It was down and dirty, raw and real. But more than that, they had the faith to encounter our Lord and receive His grace.

Faith is not a feeling but a decision to believe. It is an act of the will. Sometimes I think we are looking for warm fuzzy feelings before we reach out to Jesus. If so, we may be waiting a while.

We *choose* to step out of the crowd. We *decide* to call upon Jesus. And this is not just wishful thinking. We believe in a Man whom the Gospels and experience tell us won't let us down.

---

[13] Luke 8:48
[14] Matthew 9:28–29.

The beauty of this kind of raw and real faith is that it isn't just in regard to our needs or brokenness. It's also a way of encountering God with our dreams and desires. Think of the saints. Here are men and women who shared their hearts with the Lord and let Him lead them through the wildest adventures one could ever imagine.

I think of St. Ignatius of Loyola, who used all his intellect and imagination first to encounter Jesus and then to serve Him with creativity and zeal. Or St. Teresa of Ávila, who found in Jesus her closest friend and spent her whole life passionately planting monasteries all around Spain.

I love the saints. They show us that serving God and being human are not incompatible. They demonstrate by the example of their lives that the gifts God has given us are to be used for the building up of His Kingdom.

This, for sure, comes in many shapes and sizes. But man was made to glorify God. We do so primarily by being fully the men and women He has created us to be as well as by serving Him *with all our heart, soul, mind, and strength.*[15]

What if all the cowboys and professional people out there *sought first the Kingdom of God?*[16] What if we used all the skills and energy it took to excel in our fields and directed them to the building up of God's Kingdom? Not only would the world be a better place: we'd all be a lot happier too.

I dream of this world. Most people think that being Catholic is boring and restricted. I'm here to tell you otherwise. Catholicism is about being fully human. It's about encountering and following

---

[15]   Mark 12:30.
[16]   Matthew 6:33.

the prototypical Man, Jesus, who shows us what it means to be fully alive.[17]

Not only does He show us: He helps us too. Left to ourselves, we are base at best and dead at worst. Walking in a state of grace, however, allows the life of Christ to dwell in us.

Sure, there are dark forces out there wanting to keep us down. But Jesus dispels the darkness and gives us wings to fly. He is our perfect role model and hero. He trod the path of childlike serious-ness with a raw and real faith. And if we keep our eyes fixed on Him, He'll teach us to do the same.

[17] See John 10:10

Sonship

If I were to summarize Jesus' entire gospel message into two words, they would be *Our Father*. Jesus came to lead us back to our Father. It sounds simplistic, which, in its essence, it is. But for Him to accomplish this work, it took a lot of sacrifice.

Original Sin kicked us out of right relationship with God. But because of Jesus' victory over death, that relationship has been restored. Now, by virtue of our Baptism, Jesus is our Brother, which makes His Father our Father too.

I love pondering the Trinity. It is a mystery for sure, one to be explored, not comprehended. But at its core lies one God in three Persons: Father, Son, and Holy Spirit. Jesus is the only-begotten Son. In other words, He is fully God in the expression of being a Son. A son cannot exist without a father. Therefore, the truest identify of Jesus comes from His relationship to the Father as His Son.

It's no different for us. Because of Him, the heart of our identity as baptized Christians is found in our relationship with God the Father. Baptism incorporates us into the Body of Christ. It is a spiritual rebirth.

Now, when God the Father gazes upon you and me, He doesn't just see Ted, Suzie, or Bill. He sees the image of His Son Jesus. From there comes our individual and personal nature as male and female.

This is foundational to who we are as Christians. And just as the foundation of a house is its most crucial component, so too the rock of our Baptism is the most fundamental reality of our Christian identity.

If we build our relationship with God on this solid footing, the rest of our home will stand pretty and weather any storm. Any other foundation will set our spiritual house on shifting sand and allow it to collapse when times get tough.

This baptismal bedrock of our spiritual life is *sonship*. It is life set on the rock of Jesus Christ. Just as Jesus had the unshakable confidence that He was God's beloved Son, so can we. And not only so *can* we, but so should we!

Whether we feel it or not, or choose to believe it or not, it is absolutely true. Nothing we can do, or even God can do, can erase the baptismal brand we received as His beloved sons. Sure, we can choose not to live out of it and can even choose to hurt or sever, through sin, our relational ties to God. But the reality remains the same. We are His beloved sons.

Sonship is the good news of the Gospels. Jesus took on our flesh in order to redeem it and lead us back into right relationship with the Father. He did this primarily through His Incarnation. But in a particular way we see this manifested in the Man's own baptism.

You know the scene. Jesus is on the bank of the Jordan River with a few of His buddies, while His cousin John the Baptist is baptizing. Eventually it's our Lord's turn, and John reluctantly dunks Him. When Jesus comes out of the water, John sees the heavens open up and the Spirit descending upon Him like a dove; and the Father's voice from Heaven was heard: *You are my beloved son, with whom I am well pleased.*[18]

A connection that may be a little less known is what happens directly after. Mark's Gospel points out in the very next verse that *the Spirit immediately drove him out into the wilderness.*[19] There Jesus was tempted by Satan. And Luke's account suggests that during this time the devil threw at Him *every temptation known to mankind.*[20]

But Matthew highlights that the first two temptations of Jesus are attacks on His Sonship. Satan begins those temptations with "If you are the Son of God,"[21] and Jesus blows both out of the water by quoting the truth of Scripture against the devil's lies. The point is that the fundamental attack of Satan against Jesus is to undermine the reality that He is the Son.

If Satan can weaken the foundation upon which Jesus stands, then it's just a matter of time before the rest of His fortress begins to crumble. But Satan is no match for Jesus. The Man is humanly set on the solid rock of sonship because of the words He just heard spoken to Him by His Father: *You are my beloved son, with whom I am well pleased.*

This scene is at the beginning of Jesus' public ministry. Once He leaves the desert, He's mission-bound. His entire focus becomes gathering disciples and proclaiming the Kingdom of God. This charge of His has its great culmination on the Cross, where He reveals to the fullest extent that He is the Messiah, the Savior of the world.

---

[18]   Mark 1:11.
[19]   Mark 1:12.
[20]   See Luke 4:13.
[21]   Matthew 4:3,6.

Our Lord's mission as Messiah is not divorced from His identity as Son. The two are intrinsically intertwined. But there is a hierarchy, so to speak. His vocation as Savior of the world stems from the reality that He is God's beloved Son.

It is from this perspective of love that He fulfills the Father's will perfectly. Love propels Him. Without the firm knowledge of His Father's paternal love, I think it would have been humanly impossible for Jesus to complete His mission of dying on the Cross.

Mission comes from relationship. And the beauty of this properly ordered life is a joyful heart. In John's Gospel, we see our Lord praying before He is arrested and crucified. A rather peaceful image of a man about to die is presented.

Jesus says to His dad, "Father, the hour has come; glorify your Son that the Son may glorify you.... But now I am coming to you; and these things I speak in the world, that they may have my joy fulfilled in themselves."[22] Peace and joy are the fruits of living from the heart of sonship.

Our Lord wants to share His joy with us. But the process is not magical. It requires discipline. The same kind of discipline He shows by choosing to live out of His identity as a beloved Son of the Father. Jesus teaches us by His example but also promises to help along the way.

I don't think the knowledge of sonship is too hard to understand. Putting it into practice, however, is another story. It requires that long, arduous journey of getting out of my head and into my heart.

The heart is where this reality resides. It is believing, not just knowing, that I am God's beloved son. It is experiencing in my

[22] See John 17:1,13.

humanity, just as Jesus did, that God is my Father and, once I've experienced His love in my heart, staying there!

This truth is nothing new in Christian piety. However, the Catholic Cowboy Way to sonship is unique. It is a raw and real faith that encounters the person of Jesus Christ through our humanity.

I have never felt more like a son than in doing the things I love—ranching, in particular. There's just something about the smell of the air and the feel of the dirt that brings me to my roots. And when I allow nature to draw me back to the Author of life Himself, it's a taste of Heaven. It's incarnational. It makes me feel whole, body and soul.

One of the greatest tendencies of our fallen human nature is to be dualistic, to live as if our body and soul were separate. Catholic anthropology has always seen the human person as being composed of both body and soul. The two are intrinsically united, and if either one were missing the human person would cease to exist in this life.

We can, however, *distinguish* between our bodies and souls, just as I can distinguish my hand from my foot. But my hand and my foot are still part of my one body. In the same way, our body and soul are part of the one human person.

This understanding is important because what I do with my body affects my soul, and what I do with my soul affects my body. All of this then reflects in my humanity, for good or ill.

I love working. From the time I was a kid, watching my dad and uncles sweat and grunt, I was set upon *glorifying God with my body*.[23] All these desires were eventually fulfilled when I hit the workforce fulltime at eighteen.

[23]   1 Corinthians 6:20.

My uncle who employed me was great. He stood me up on the two pillars of responsibility and creativity. He would show me how to do things, but the next time around, it was up to me. I had to improvise.

Suddenly a part of me awoke. We drove tow trucks at the time, and when there was a vehicle rolled over in the bottom of a creek, it was up to me to get it out. I was alone with God, and the two of us would get the job done. And boy was it fun.

We also welded a lot in the shop. Engaging my hands through my imagination became a powerful connection to the divine. Our God is creative. And when I was set free to co-create, it felt godlike.

Responsibility and creativity are two legs on which the human person is meant to stand *and run*. They, along with all the senses the Lord has given us, are ways of encountering Him through our humanity. They reveal to us our individual personality and identity. They help us to know that we are sons — and not just one of many sons but individual beloved sons of God the Father.

God has created us not only for a purpose but also with a personality. Your interests and mine may be different, but they are both avenues to encountering our Father. How easy it is to put ourselves in a box and say this is the kind of person I *should* be. Or this is what a Christian *should* look like. Not true. The only prototypical Christian is Christ Himself. After that, the sky's the limit.

Blow that box up. Become who God created you to be, and then stay there. Granted, this is not always easy work. But Jesus is here to help us discover our individual sonship.

Prayer is key to this enterprise. It is there that we hear God speak to us. When we start to tune in to the Father's voice through our humanity, then prayer becomes a continual conversation with God.

Thanks be to God, going to Mass was always a priority for me. This intimate encounter with God began to spill over into my everyday life. Suddenly I found myself talking to Someone, bouncing ideas around my head with another Person throughout the day.

Eventually it dawned on me that this was God. We were communicating in a human, natural way. But more than that, it was personal, as if He knew me better than I knew myself. And the more we conversed, the more I began to experience His love for me as His son.

I know we have all had experiences like this at various points in our lives and to varying degrees. The trick is staying there. Often we get knocked off this horse and just chalk it up to God's pulling the rug out from under us. Not so.

That is not the nature of a loving Father. He wants to visit with us at all times. However, we do have an adversary who is happy to help us not live out of our sonship. His name is Satan. He spent forty long days trying to get Jesus out of the saddle of His Sonship. And Satan spends our lifetime trying to do the same. He's also relentless.

The spiritual life is a bronc. It'll dump you if you're not careful. But if you keep your mind in the middle of sonship, it's a dance that never gets old. God wants us to live out of our identity as His beloved children at all hours and through all seasons of our lives! And the surest way to do this is by *listening to Him*.[24]

Jesus is the *Word* of the Father. God spoke, and creation happened through Jesus Christ; "He was in the beginning with God; all things were made through him, and without him was not anything made that was made."[25] This *Word made flesh* conveys the Father's intimate love for each one of us.

The trick is tuning in to that voice and tuning out of all the others. Sonship is the frequency of the Father. If we stay tuned

---

[24]   See Luke 9:35
[25]   John 1:2–3.

in to Jesus through our own humanity as beloved sons, no horse can shake us.

Experience has taught me that sonship is the surest way forward. It is not a passive path, but a creative way of fulfilling the Father's will with peace and joy. Probably the most common way for Christians to get thrown out of the saddle of sonship is through the error of *activism*—not taking time to rest in the Lord.

There is no doubt that we are called to be active in the Christian life. Jesus Himself said, "My food is to do the will of him who sent me, and to accomplish his work."[26] But He also said, "Come away by yourselves to a lonely place, and rest a while."[27] Sonship is a delicate dance for sure. But to get it right, we need to have our priorities straight.

This dynamic is illustrated no better than with Martha and Mary, Jesus' close friends. Luke's Gospel paints a picture that we are all familiar with. Jesus is at Martha and Mary's home, enjoying some friendly hospitality. Mary is sitting at His feet, while Martha is busy preparing the food.

Martha, anxious about getting dinner ready and annoyed that her sister isn't helping, lashes out and complains to Jesus. Our Lord, in His stern love, simply says, *Martha, Martha, you are anxious and troubled about many things. Only one thing is needed. Mary has chosen the better part and it shall not be taken from her.*[28] The *better part* that Mary has chosen is sonship, sitting at the feet of the Son and knowing in her heart that she is a beloved child of God.

It's not that Martha's serving is bad. In fact, it's good. The trouble is that her feathers get ruffled. She's out of the saddle of

---

[26] John 4:34.
[27] Mark 6:31.
[28] Luke 10:41–42.

sonship. Martha and Mary can be seen as two dimensions of the one person, who is each of us. By nature, we are active and contemplative, body and soul. These two dimensions are intrinsically one, but we have the tendency to divorce them.

The answer is to be *contemplatives in action*. We never leave the feet of Jesus when we go out to serve Him. We don't stop being Mary in order to become Martha.

If we do, anxiety ensues. We remain both Mary and Martha. Like a horse and rider, the two are meant to work together. But serving is not to take precedence over sitting. Working is not to usurp sonship. Work without prayer is like a body without a soul. It's dead.

This dynamic can be at play in all vocations, but especially in the priesthood. It is easy to think that my work is my prayer because it is work directly related to God. But I am still a man, and if this work doesn't derive from being a son, it easily falls into activism. It may objectively bear fruit through the grace of God, but personally I can become depleted and seek unhealthy venues to satisfy my thirsty soul.

However, when my priestly work derives from being a beloved son, then we're ranchin'! Not only am I in tune with the Holy Spirit to make more effective shots in ministry, but I also enjoy the ride.

When I constantly return to and live out of the wellspring of sonship, I happily celebrate the sacraments as well as welcome all that the encounters with the People of God can bring. My ministry has personal meaning because it is the Father, who loves me as His son, whom I am serving.

My modus operandi as a priest is that *I'm a son before I'm a father.* I'm a baptized Christian before I'm an ordained priest. The two go hand and hand and are intrinsically united. But the proper ordering is crucial.

My whole life as a priest revolves around the reality that I'm a son. Not that this disposition is new; our Lord invented it. Jesus patterned His whole life around being a son before being the Messiah. And I follow His example.

Sure, sonship looks unique on me in the twenty-first century, as it does on all of us. But I love it. Being a cowboy is part of the nature God blessed me with. And I live it out with peace, confidence, and joy. It is from this disposition and perspective that I act and serve as a priest. But I never take off my hat when I put on my collar.

It is easy to become compartmentalized and check our Baptism at the door when we act in our vocation or occupation. But life is much better when we never leave our heart as we work in the world. I'm a son before I'm a father; and so are you a son before a husband, or a daughter before a mother. If we get this right, life is fun, and we get the job done.

Sonship is a spiritual bronc. It's easy to get off to the side and land in the dirt. But the true mark of a cowboy is not if we get bucked off or not. It's whether we get back on again. We live and learn. And when we get life in Christ right, there's nothing better in the whole world.

Jesus paves the way. His whole life was centered on being a beloved Son of His heavenly Father. It's from this disposition that He acted with peace and joy as the Messiah. The same dynamic is open to all of us. The Catholic Cowboy Way of sonship is not complicated, but it does take grit. Our Father has given us a lifetime to perfect it. The way forward is simple. All we have to do is *listen to Him*.

Conversion

"Repent, for the kingdom of heaven is at hand."[29] These are the opening words of our Lord's public ministry. Talk about coming out swinging! They come fresh off His forty-day sojourn in the desert with the devil, which was immediately preceded by His baptism in the Jordan.

Listening to Jesus is not necessarily easy. Without a doubt He *has the words of eternal life*.[30] But that still doesn't make them pleasant. Repent? Who wants to repent? The truth is that none of us do. Due to our fallen human nature, we have inherited the tendency to want to do things our way, which is usually not the way of the Father.

Repentance is turning back to God and following His ways. It means to stop sinning. Sin is a decision on my part not to obey the Father, plain and simple. The word obey comes from the Latin word *obedire*, which literally means *to listen*. Minor disobedience wounds our relationship with God, while major, deliberate choices to act contrary to the Father's will can sever our relationship with Him.

---

[29] Matthew 4:17.
[30] John 6:68.

Thanks be to God for Jesus. He came to heal us and restore our relationship with the Father. The first step is repentance. Repentance is the opposite of sin. Where sin is a conscious choice to turn away from God, repentance is the deliberate decision to turn back to Him. We might simply call this dynamic *conversion*.

I remember my first notable conversion experience. I was in high school and choosing to do things my way, to say the least. Along with being on the wrong side of the law, this was probably the unhappiest point in my life. It all came to a head one day, and my sin was laid bare for all to see. Two roads lay ahead of me: to stay in the mire and muck or turn and follow the Father.

It's hard to explain the tough grace I experienced in that moment. On one hand was the shame of the sin. But on the other was the hope for a brighter future. The decision was up to me, though. God was inviting, but I had to make the firm resolve to repent of the sin and be open to His grace.

One significant moment in this experience was Dad's hand on my shoulder. I knew he had my back. He always has. But something deeper was going on too. The new horizons opening up to me pointed beyond my earthly father to my Heavenly Father. In that moment, I knew what I had to do. It might not be easy, but my dads—one down here, One up there—would help me along the right way.

As in all conversions, this was not a one-and-done sort of thing. With God's grace, I took a step in the right direction, which necessarily required me to cut off those things that were leading me down the wrong road. But after that first step, there was a second step, and a third, and so on, each one requiring a conscious, deliberate choice on my part to choose the good.

For sure, this process of spiritual maturing was not textbook. It was more like the school of hard knocks. We all learn as we go, but the call to *repent and believe in the kingdom of God* is always at hand. I call this *continual conversion*. True conversion is never once-and-done. Our relationship with God is always a work in progress.

Following the Father is traveling down the *good road*. When He created the world, He saw that *everything was good*. What does it mean to be good? Goodness is when things act in accordance with their nature, or when things follow their intended purpose. In the case of human persons, we are good when we act according to the nature and purpose we are created with.

This goes back to before the Fall, when all of creation was properly ordered because it followed the logical purpose God designed it with. The world became disordered when man, in his free will, chose to act contrary to God's design. Through our free will, we sinned, and evil entered the world. Because of this, traveling down the good road is difficult for us, and left to ourselves, we are inclined not to choose it.

But the good road is where we find freedom and happiness. It is the road to living a purposeful life. It is what man is created for, and he can find fulfillment only when he consciously chooses the good.

We call this firm and habitual disposition to choose the good a *virtue*. The word *virtue* derives from Latin word *vir*, which means *man*. Man is fully himself when he acts virtuously, when choosing the good becomes second nature.

Virtue is the way of living continual conversion. Repentance gets us straight in the saddle, and virtue is how we ride. No doubt, Jesus' call to turn back to God is something we always must heed. But once we are heading in the right direction, virtue is the way forward. It's when boys become men.

After high school, when I moved to Montana, my cousin came to visit. At one point in our conversation, I recalled how intense it was when he used to cut weight for wrestling. We would have a Thanksgiving feast at Grandma's house, and he would only eat salad. He acknowledged the craziness of this, and then he said, "But I miss the discipline."

Discipline, the only way to grow in virtue. Take any unbroken horse; the only way to make it rideable is to discipline it. In our culture, discipline gets a bad rap. It can be looked on as harsh and hard, and it *can* be if it's done with ill intentions and to try to conform something into what it's not meant to be.

But the flip side of discipline is flourishing. Left to himself, my horse would still be a wild stud, getting in trouble, and would have only minimal skills that come from breeding and survival. But with a little charitable discipline, he is now calm and cool, can drag calves to the fire for branding, and gets his picture posted all over Facebook for jumping in back of my pickup. Thanks to discipline, Chief now flourishes as a horse instead of simply surviving as a wild beast.

It's no different for us. If our passions run the show, we are basically animals, slaves to our stomachs and testicles. But with a little discipline, we can become gentlemen: free men who are in control of ourselves. And what's cool about us is that we don't have to be castrated to get there. We have free will. Truly *free* will wants to choose the good. But to get to that point of virtue, we have to discipline our passions.

I think the first chastisement I took on was food and drink. Gluttony has always been considered a vice, which is the opposite of a virtue. But it is so because it causes my hunger and thirst to control me, not the other way around. When I haphazardly give in to the whims of my stomach, I am less of a man. Don't get me wrong; food and drink are important to both survival and flourishing. But left unchecked, hunger and thirst can lead to slavery. The virtue of temperance, which helps us to avoid excess and extremes, calms the passions. Temperance is obtainable to everyone, but only through discipline.

Often when we want to grow in a virtue, we have to go above and beyond in the opposite direction and then land in the middle, where we want to be. For me, this came through fasting. I first discovered the value of fasting as a young man during Lent. The Church has always encouraged us to practice some sort of fast on Fridays. During Lent, this takes the form of abstinence from meat. So I simply took it a step further and just didn't eat the whole day. Turns out it can be done. And not only that: fasting for a day frees the mind.

This kind of rigor was not harsh punishment but discipline. It began to teach my passions that they were not in control; I was. Slowly the virtue of temperance began to develop in my life, and I began to walk freer. This allowed me then to tackle other loose ends in my life as well, such as the use of alcohol. I've always enjoyed a cold beer, but fasting from alcohol over Lent taught me that moderation is necessary when it comes to drinking.

Virtues are always a saddle to stay in the middle of. Once they are obtained, they need to be maintained. I still enjoy food and drink, but I do so temperately. I try to always be conscientious in deciding at what times I eat and how much. I try to keep drinking to its proper time and place as well, and that includes choosing never to get drunk. But fasting from these goods is often still necessary to make sure it is I riding the horse and not my passions riding me.

Virtue leads to virtue. The more we grow in one virtue, the more doors open up to others. The most freeing virtue I've ever experienced is chastity. I am a chaste celibate man, but that discipline isn't natural. It's supernatural. Celibacy is for intimacy with God. And through it, and with the help of His grace, I am able to dedicate 100 percent of my being to God. Not only am I humanly fulfilled by His continual presence, but celibacy is the reason I'm able to be a wildcat for God.

Yet the freedom of celibacy is unattainable without the virtue of chastity. Chastity is the natural virtue for everyone. Whether we're a teenager, a single person, married, or celibate, chastity is the universal virtue that governs our sexual passions.

Again, things are good when they follow their natural order. And the natural purpose of the sexual act is twofold: the unity of persons and the procreation of children.[31] If either one of these elements is missing, sexuality turns bad and we sin, leading us away from God and true happiness.

It's pretty simple. The sexual act leads to a communion of committed persons who have entered into a covenantal marriage bond with each other. It is also intended by God for the generation of children and therefore requires an openness to conception. Hence, its purpose is for the uniting of married couples in deeper communion with each other and for the co-creation of new life, be it God's will that the couple conceive.

All this points to the reality that if I'm not married or open to new life, the sexual act is off-limits in any way, shape, or form. To modern man, this sounds like white-knuckled hell. But to the virtuously chaste, it is freedom.

Why? Because my sexual passions don't control me; *I* control them. It is the rider being in control of the horse and not vice versa. And when horse and rider, my sexuality and I, work in communion, there is a synergy that glorifies God and fulfills His will.

---

[31] See Pope St. Paul VI, encyclical *Humanae Vitae* (July 25, 1968), no. 12.

As with the rest of fallen humanity, chastity did not come easy to me. I had to work at it in cooperation with God's grace. That task can seem daunting if we look too far ahead. But virtues are best won by taking one right step after another.

Let's start with Jesus and His Sermon on the Mount. Our Lord says, "Every one who looks at a woman lustfully has already committed adultery with her in his heart."[32] This is baseline chastity. If we get true custody of the eyes right, freedom is just a hop, skip, and a jump away. But if we don't, we will be perpetual slaves to our sexual passions.

Our current culture gives us plenty of opportunity to practice this discipline. And our Lord is here to help as well. But we have to do our part. Back in my day, it would be considered ridiculous if I wanted to stop looking at pornography but wasn't willing to throw out the magazines. The same goes for today. It would be absurd to think I could kick a porn addiction without throwing away my smartphone.

The truth can hurt, but it can also set us free. Think of an airplane. It has to face into the wind to take off and fly. If we honestly face our vices and sins head-on in truth, God will help set us free. And for Christians, truth is not just a concept; it's a person, Jesus Christ. And not only is the truth a person; it is also a church. As St. Paul says, the Church is the "pillar and bulwark of truth."[33]

I feel that I've always known Jesus in one way or another. I may not have always listened to Him, but I always knew Him. My family made sure we went to Mass every Sunday and I also had plenty of good examples of Christian living. But I can honestly say that I really didn't know Christ's Church until later in life.

[32] Matthew 5:28.
[33] 1 Timothy 3:15.

In my mid-twenties, I worked on a ranch in Montana. I was hauling hay one afternoon when I received a phone call from my aunt, who was Baptist. This is a woman whom I dearly love, but that afternoon I got an earful of why I was going to Hell for being Catholic. I was shocked by her presumptions about the Catholic Faith and was honestly hurt when she said I wasn't a Christian. But what was more disappointing is that I didn't have an answer to her condemnations.

"Why does the Catholic Church teach what she does?" I thought to myself. "Lord, please help me discover the truth about Christianity," I prayed. Now, I wasn't much of a reader, so to pick up the *Catechism of the Catholic Church* was not a viable option. One Sunday, however, the Lord answered my prayer when I saw an ad in the Church bulletin for a local EWTN radio station. My life was about to change forever.

I tuned in, and I couldn't believe my ears. It was the truth! The faith and reason that poured out of those speakers went through my ears, into my mind, and took root in my heart. I remember listening to EWTN while baling hay. Stepping out of the tractor, I threw my hands into the air, praising God for the truth that was setting me free! Listening to Catholic radio set me on fire with the wisdom of the Catholic Church—so much so, that I left the ranch and went to the seminary.

Catholicism is the fullness of Christianity. Does this mean that only Catholics are going to Heaven? No. Jesus "desires all men to be saved and to come to the knowledge of truth."[34] Does it mean that Catholics are perfect Christians? Not necessarily. I know plenty of non-Catholic Christians who put my faith to shame.

But we do not throw the baby out with the bath water. What are the historical facts about Christianity? What does the Catholic

---

[34] 1 Timothy 2:4.

Church actually teach and why? I dare you to seek the answers to these questions.

Continual conversion doesn't stop with turning away from sin and growing in virtue. St. Paul says, "Do not be conformed to this world but be transformed by the renewal of your mind."[35] We are intelligent beings and put our minds to work in all sorts of tasks.

How about the Faith? If God is the source of all creation, wouldn't that mean that our faith in Him is also rational? After all, creation itself is logical. Reason is a way of knowing God and diving deep into our Faith.

Sure, I was born Catholic, but today I choose to practice Catholicism. The second half of our Lord's opening proclamation to the world and His call to repentance, was *for the kingdom of heaven is at hand.* I am fully convinced that the Catholic Church is the presence of that kingdom on earth. In fact, Church theology and documents support such a thought.

The Second Vatican Council document *Lumen Gentium* states: "To carry out the will of the Father Christ inaugurated the Kingdom of heaven on earth and revealed to us his mystery.... The Church—that is the kingdom of Christ already present in mystery—grows visibly through the power of God in the world."[36] The Church is this mystery of Christ because she contains the presence of Christ.

Our Lord says, *I will be with you always, even until the end of time.*[37] This is not an idea but a reality. We have seven sacraments in the Catholic Church. The word *sacrament* derives from the Greek

---

[35] Romans 12:2.
[36] Second Vatican Council, Dogmatic Constitution on the Church *Lumen Gentium* (November 21, 1964), no. 3.
[37] Matthew 28:20.

word for mystery. The sacraments are sacred signs instituted by Christ to give grace.[38] This grace is the power of Christ's presence continuing to work in the word. His Kingdom has already come, through the Church!

There are many reasons why I am Catholic and why I have no doubt that the Catholic Church is the Church that Christ established. She has the authority given by Christ to teach and govern through apostolic succession, especially that of Peter. She has a liturgical worship that is an extension of Jewish ceremony as well as that of the early Church. But the greatest reason that I am Catholic is because of the Eucharist.

The Eucharist is the *source and summit* of our Catholic Faith.[39] Being one of the seven sacraments, the Eucharist is the *Real Presence* of Jesus still on earth, hidden under the veil of bread and wine. The word *Eucharist* literally means *thanksgiving*. In gratitude, then, the Eucharist is a memorial offering to the Father for Jesus' Passion, death, and Resurrection, which continues to save us.

The theology of this is deep, to say the least. But what struck me so many years ago, and still does, is that Jesus, in His humanity and divinity, is still with us in every Catholic church throughout the world. Chew on that reality for a while.

I remember the first time I really read the sixth chapter of John's Gospel. Our Lord's words blew my mind—especially when Jesus said:

> Truly, truly, I say to you, unless you eat the flesh of the Son of man and drink his blood, you have no life in you; he who eats my flesh and drinks my blood has eternal life, and I

---

[38] See the *Catechism of the Catholic Church* (CCC), no. 1131.

[39] *Catechism of the Catholic Church* (CCC), no. 1324, quoting *Lumen Gentium* 11.

will raise him up at the last day. For my flesh is food indeed and my blood is drink indeed. He who eats my flesh and drinks my blood abides in me, and I in him.[40]

Jesus is literally the bread of life.

For many in Jesus' day, this was a hard teaching.[41] And for many in our day, this continues to be a tough teaching. But what if it were true? What if Jesus continues to be literally present on this earth in the Blessed Sacrament of the Eucharist? Well, I'm here to tell you that it is true. How do I know? Because I've experienced Him.

Theologically speaking, we know God through His effects. There is an occasion where I might wonder whether Jesus is really present in the Eucharist or whether, as a priest, I can actually bring that presence about. But then I think of the transformation that has gone on in my life after years of receiving Holy Communion with faith and in a state of grace. I can honestly say with St. Paul, *it is no longer I who live, but Christ who lives in me.*[42]

The Catholic Church is the Immaculate Bride of Christ. She is perfect. Her members, you and I, are not. I love her and have given my life to her, as a husband gives his life to his wife. I know that many struggle with her, and I have fought that fight as well. But I'm here to tell you; Catholicism is the fullness of Christianity. She is Heaven on earth.

Repent, for the kingdom of heaven is at hand. There is more here to Jesus' opening words than meets the eye. Sure, it involves conversion. But more than that, it involves *continual* conversion, always seeking the truth.

[40] John 6:53–56.
[41] See John 6:60–66.
[42] Galatians 2:20.

The first place to start is with sin. *Go and sin no more,*[43] our Lord tells the many whom He has had mercy on. Sin wounds our relationship with the Father and can even sever it. Resisting sin is the first step to a right relationship with God.

But it doesn't stop there. We continue to mature in that relationship, and virtue is the standard way of doing so. Virtue is the path to true freedom. It is the healthy habit of choosing the good, which makes man flourish. But to grow in virtue takes discipline. With our effort, in cooperation with God's grace, the virtuous man is the truly happy man.

The destination of all this conversion is Heaven. However, we don't have to wait until we die to experience Heaven. Christ's heavenly Kingdom can be found on earth in the Catholic Church. This is primarily because His Real Presence remains in the Eucharist, which is housed and celebrated in every Catholic church throughout the world.

Everyone's path of conversion is unique. What's described in this book is the way the Lord has led *this* cowboy. But I think we'd be hard-pressed to say that any of these elements—repentance, virtue, and seeking the truth—can be excluded in a true conversion to Christ. Continual conversion keeps us in a right relationship with the Father through listening to His Son Jesus, who dwells in our hearts through the Holy Spirit. But this is only the beginning. After we have heard Him, then it's time to follow Him.

[43] See John 5:14; 8:11.

Discipleship

Once Jesus showed the world His cards in His inaugural address, He spent the next three years teaching people His way. Being the author of human nature, He knew that men learn best through hands-on experience and over the course of time. So He began to call *followers*, men and women who would walk with Him and learn from Him how to be Christians.

To learn by following is called *discipleship*. This was nothing new in Jesus' day, and it's nothing new today. We learn by example. There are apprenticeships in almost all occupations, times when people are taught the tricks of the trade before they bust out on their own. It is similar with our Lord, except that the education never ends.

The word *disciple* means *student*. We become students of Christianity by following Jesus and learning from Him. But the beauty of this kind of school is that it is not rote. We don't become cookie-cutter Christians. Christianity looks unique on all of us. Sure, it has the same doctrine, principles, and morals. But the way Christ looks on each of us is totally personal.

Throughout the Gospels Jesus calls men and women to follow Him. There is probably no more classic scene than the one that comes directly after His opening lines to the world. Our Lord is walking along the beaches of Galilee and sees Simon and his brother Andrew fishing. He says to them: " 'Follow me, and I will make you fishers of men.' Immediately they left their nets and followed him."[44]

What I love about this scene is that it encompasses all the aspects of true discipleship. First, Matthew's inclusion of the boys' names suggests that our Lord already knew them personally. They weren't just random good ole boys who He thought would make decent hands. No, He knew them intimately even before He called them.

A calling from God has traditionally been known as a *vocation*. The word *vocation* comes from the Latin verb *vocare*, which means *to call*. The current use of the word usually has to do with the bigger states in life, such as marriage or the priesthood. However, vocation is a general mode of discipleship. God calls and we follow.

I like to speak about the *universal call to discipleship*. This is the perennial vocation for all of us. From the time we are baptized until the day they lay us in the ground, we are called to be Jesus' disciples. This is good news because those who are not married or entered into the consecrated life often wonder what their vocation is. Their vocation is to discipleship! And from there we can discern our bigger call to a particular state in life.

The truth is, Jesus calls each of us by name to follow Him and to learn from Him. Our Lord knows human nature perfectly. After all, He is the author of it. But deeper than that, He knows our individual human nature perfectly. He knows exactly what will make us flourish. We are uniquely different, but collectively we

---

[44] Matthew 4:19–20.

need to learn from the same master. Jesus teaches us to become fully the Christian men and women He created us to be.

This is possible only by being a disciple of Jesus. The Second Vatican Council document *Gaudium et Spes* emphasizes this when it states: "The truth is that only in the mystery of the incarnate Word does the mystery of man take on light."[45] By following Jesus and learning from Him, we learn to be fully ourselves. In Him is not only the prototype of perfect humanity in general, but also the mystery of our individual human fulfillment.

The second part of Jesus' *calling* of Simon and Andrew on the shores of Galilee is that they were fishermen. Our Lord calls all men and women to discipleship, but He seems to have a fondness for the blue-collar workers. Why? Probably because, by and large, they are down-to-earth folks. In the raw and realness of everyday life, peasants often have more of an openness to hearing and following God.

It doesn't matter, though, what our occupation is or what our talents may be. The point is that Jesus wants to perfect them and use them for God's greater glory. Simon and Andrew were fishermen. And over the course of their time spent with Jesus, He taught them how to catch bigger *fish*: men. Jesus doesn't destroy human nature; He perfects it.

Properly ordered, our gifts and interest serve God and our brothers and sisters. And when they do, we also find fulfillment. However, without the guiding hand of the Author of every good gift, man typically uses his gifts to build his own kingdom, not God's. The Father gave us talents to be used for His greater glory and the building up of His kingdom. By following Jesus, we can learn this art.

---

[45] Second Vatican Council Pastoral Constitution on the Church in the Modern World *Gaudium et Spes* (December 7, 1965), no. 22.

But none of these fruits of discipleship are possible unless we fully surrender ourselves to Jesus. The third part of Jesus' call to the boys on the banks of the Sea of Galilee is their complete surrender to Him: *they left their nets and followed Him.* They were all in. And leaving their livelihood behind symbolizes that.

Fully surrendering our lives to Christ is a lifelong project. But there are some milestones along the way, the first being our Baptism. In Baptism, we spiritually died and were reborn in Christ. From that moment on, full-on following Jesus is the program. But often that call gets drowned out by worldly ambitions, and we take the reins of our lives back into own hands.

Our Lord never stops calling us to follow Him, though. He is the *Hound of Heaven.* But even in an intentional walk with Him, there are mile markers of surrender. The one in my life that stands out the most is when I left for seminary. In fact, dying is the only way to describe it.

Life was good at twenty-eight. I was ranching full-time and was happy to do so for the rest of my life. But the priesthood was looming in the background. I had thought of it before but was hesitant. It wasn't celibacy; that would be easy compared with going back to school. I hated schoolwork; that's why I didn't go to college after high school.

Ranching was my gig. It was there that I could utilize all the skills and gifts the Lord had blessed me with: cowboying, farming, fabricating. Besides that, I was engaged to the rancher's daughter. Life was as good as it could get, but my heart was restless. The desire to walk away from everything and serve the Lord alone was deep in my heart.

One day, the Lord broke through in prayer and revealed to me His call to the priesthood. I stood up in amazement and knew what I had to do. It was time to go all in with God. It was time to die. There has been no more determining moment in my life than leaving the girl of my dreams, on the ranch of my dreams, in order to follow the God of my dreams. It was a decisive step in my discipleship that I'm forever grateful God gave me the grace to take.

Discipleship is dying to self in order to live for Christ. That sounds harsh, but it is what we are made for. We are created to love and be loved. Love, in its essence, is a total gift of self. Jesus shows us this on the Cross: *no greater love has a man than to lay down his life for his friends.*[46] Surrendering our lives to Christ and committing to following Him is a great act of love.

We are born to die. It's the only thing we can all count on in this life. The sooner we come to terms with that, the happier we will be. In fact, we don't have to wait until our death to die. We are given opportunities all throughout our lives to give of ourselves out of love. Again, in her document *Gaudium et Spes*, the Church teaches us that man "cannot fully find himself except through a sincere gift of himself" (no. 24). It is in giving of ourselves that we find ourselves.

Our Lord Himself says: "If any man would come after me, let him deny himself and take up his cross and follow me. For whoever would save his life will lose it; and whoever loses his life for my sake and the gospel's will save it."[47] Jesus teaches us how to love properly, which is losing ourselves for the good of the other. Our fallen human nature is selfish, which is hellish because it can never be satisfied. But if we daily deny ourselves and follow Christ, He will teach us the path to true life.

Giving of ourselves for the good of God and neighbor is where real life begins. This is contrary to what the world teaches us. But

[46] John 15:13.
[47] Mark 8:34–35.

giving of ourselves out of love is a putting to death of the selfish self. It is also freedom because nothing can harm us because we've already died. I think the inscription over an old monastery in Greece puts it well: *If you die before you die, when you die, you will never die.* Death is the secret to life. It is in dying that we learn to live.

Again, Jesus teaches us how to do both. He modeled how to give fully of ourselves when He surrendered Himself to the Father on the Cross. And He showed us that such love leads to life in the Resurrection. This is the school of discipleship that Jesus invites us all to. The only prerequisite is that we go *all in* with Him.

Granted, full-on discipleship looks unique on all of us. That's the beauty of it. But it's hard to deny that our Lord is calling all of us to drop our nets and follow Him in one way or another. As He Himself says, *Unless you hate your father and mother... even your own life, you cannot be my disciple.*[48] In other words, nothing can get in our way of following Christ.

This also is not a once-and-done action. We continue to grow deeper in that relationship. We became disciples at our Baptism, but we have to continually choose to live out that reality.

Cool. Count me in. But what does that look like today, two thousand years after the Man died, rose, and ascended back to Heaven? How do I discover Jesus and follow Him with *all my heart, soul, mind, and strength?* The answer is not complicated. Discipleship *is following the voice of God in our hearts.*

Jesus is not an imaginary friend. He is not a figurative person that we learn about only in Sunday school. He's alive! And He lives in our hearts through the Holy Spirit.

After Jesus' Resurrection, He ascended back to Heaven. His disciples were perplexed as to why He was leaving. But He consoled

---

[48]   Luke 14:26.

them by saying, *It is good that I go so that I can send you the Spirit.*[49] Our Lord Jesus may have physically left this earth, but He continues to be spiritually present to us by His Spirit dwelling in our hearts.

For me, this is probably the most fun part about being a disciple of Christ. Following Him is not a dry set of rules and prescriptions. It is dynamic! Jesus speaks to our hearts and inspires us to follow Him through our heart's desires.

This almost sounds too good to be true. You mean God actually wants me to do what I want to do? Yep. If our hearts are properly ordered, God the Father motivates us to follow His Son Jesus through the Holy Spirit dwelling in our hearts.

A properly ordered heart is key here. This is why all of the dying and surrendering stuff is so crucial to our walk with Christ. It straightens up our priorities. Instead of my world revolving around me, in true discipleship my world revolves around God.

The beauty is that this is what we are made for. When my life becomes centered on God's love for me and my desire becomes to fulfill His will, then we're ranchin'! This is what being Christlike is all about. When Jesus and I are in communion, I start to think and act like Him.

Seminary was good for me. In a sense, it was like the bootcamp tactic of breaking you down in order to build you up. By leaving everything behind, I was able to start fresh with God. Slowly, good things were given back to me along with the motivating factor to use them for God's greater glory and to fulfill His will.

At one point on this journey, I remember praying, "Father, I desire to do Your will." To which He responded, "Your desire is my will." How fascinating! *I desire to do Your will. Your desire is my will.* Why not? I can think of no better way to motivate a person

---

[49] John 16:7.

than to inspire them from within. God is so amazing! It's like He made us or something.

Slowly I started to bring back the tools. Little by little, one small project after another, I learned that my desire to be creative with wood and metal were not something to be ignored but something to be pursued. They were ways of glorifying God and building up His Kingdom. Everything I gave up, He was giving back in some way, shape, or form. It reminded me of the psalm: "Take delight in the LORD, and he will give you the desires of your heart."[50]

No doubt this takes discernment. We don't just act on every fancy that comes our way. We discern it. In a nutshell, spiritual discernment is the distinguishing between spirits. We are spiritual people and we live in a spiritual world. But there are good spirits and there are bad spirits. Discernment allows us to distinguish between them in order to accept the good spirits and reject the bad ones.

This discipline of discernment is a science all its own. St. Ignatius of Loyola discovered it, and many authors since then have expanded on it. But I feel I've been able to boil down discernment of the heart to a quick gut check to help ensure that we are following the Spirit of Christ and not the spirit of the enemy, Satan.

Jesus is the truth.[51] And the truth is not complicated, but getting there can be. So our simple discernment checklist focuses on what the Spirit of Christ in our hearts sounds like. Once we have that foundation set, it will be easier to distinguish all the other spirits that don't measure up, so that we can reject them and follow the desires that do.

---

[50] Psalm 37:4.
[51] See John 14:6.

The first criterion as to whether the desires of my heart match the voice of God is whether they are *in accord with Church teaching*. This is crucial, because, as St. Paul says, Jesus is "the head of the body, the Church."[52] When we listen to the Church, we listen to Christ. When we don't, we don't. Jesus will never motivate us to do something outside the teachings of His Church. He will never inspire you to cheat on your wife. Reject that spirit; it's from the enemy.

However, if the initial examination of our heart's desire is in accord with the teachings of the Catholic Church, we can move on to the next court of discernment. Is this desire I'm experiencing *long-standing*? No doubt the Holy Spirit can inspire us to move quickly and certainly does at times. But in the course of our normal discipleship with Jesus, the Holy Spirit usually motivates us slowly. Over time, our Godly desires reveal to us His call to action.

This is a critical component in discerning God's voice because impulse desires are usually not from God. How many of us have had buyer's remorse over a pickup we thought we just had to have? Desires that are from God have a perpetual presence to them. As I discern them, I can see a thread that has been there to some degree over a long period, maybe even years. This same thread doesn't come and go. It is consistently there.

Sometimes desires of the heart can really fire us up. However, the discerned desires that come from God do not necessarily resemble fire. Fire is volatile and waxes and wanes. Desires from God are consistent, like a thirst. Think of our Lord. He wasn't impulsive, but He was driven from the get-go to fulfill the Father's

---

[52] Colossians 1:18.

will. Inspired desires drive us forward until they are quenched in the fulfillment of the Father's will.

The final criterion in a disciple's discernment of his heart's desires is its *fruit*. What fruit does this spiritual desire bear in my heart? St. Paul says in his Letter to the Galatians that the fruits of the Holy Spirit are "love, joy, peace, patience, kindness, goodness, faithfulness, gentleness, self-control."[53] In other words, this is how the voice of the Holy Spirit resonates in our hearts.

Our Lord says *you can know a tree by its fruit*.[54] A perfect example of this comes through discerning the origin of our hearts' desires. Am I being motivated by peace or fear? This is critical. Believe it or not, we are often convinced that fear is worth following. Tread lightly, though; fear is not a fruit of the Holy Spirit.

Beyond that, fear is the favorite tactic of the devil to get us off our discipleship track. Fear is an emotion, not a desire from the heart. It has its place if a bear is chasing me down. But outside of that, Jesus says, *Do not be afraid*.[55] Cowboys don't follow fear.

They do follow love, joy, and peace, though. This is the voice of the Holy Spirit, and we can have a discerned confidence that when we hear the fruits of the Spirit, we are following the Lord. In summary: peace accept, fear reject.

There are those times when the Lord calls us to do things that we don't want to do. But generally speaking, in these moments there is still the presence of the spiritual fruits even when our bodies are hesitant. Think of our Lord in the Garden of Gethsemane. Trembling, He still carried out His mission in peace.

---

[53] Galatians 5:22–23.
[54] Luke 6:44.
[55] See John 6:20 for example.

This cowboy way of discerning from the hip is not infallible. We are very capable of convincing ourselves of anything. But it does give us guidelines to know whether the voice in our hearts comes from God or not.

Over time we can have confidence in following Christ through our hearts' desires if they are *in accord with Church teaching,* if they are *long-standing,* and if they bear the *fruit of the Holy Spirit.* If any one of these elements is missing, I would be very hesitant to move onward.

Discipleship is the Catholic Cowboy Way forward. All of humanity is called to it. But the beauty is that this hat looks unique on all of us. Jesus calls us by name to follow Him. He knows our gifts and interests, and He doesn't want to destroy them. He wants to perfect them.

The one prerequisite for us all, though, is to go all in with Him. None of us is excluded from *dropping our nets and following Him.* How that looks on you and me is between us and God.

This is when life gets fun, though. Believe it or not, God wants us to be happy. And He knows the way to get us there, by following His Son. Jesus is not a figment of our imagination; He is a living person who dwells in our hearts through the Holy Spirit. In a properly ordered life, we follow Jesus by following the discerned desires of our hearts.

Discipleship is the everlasting ranch truck that the Catholic Cowboy drives through this life. It fits us personally, and it will never let us down. Besides being fun, it is our means of getting the job done. The next step in life's great adventure is the highway of holiness that we travel down.

Holiness

In 2009, Pope Benedict XVI inaugurated the Year of the Priest. At the conclusion of that year, he had an audience with all the priests who came to Rome, and they were able to ask him questions. My buddy was at that gathering, and what struck him the most was how the Holy Father answered the questions.

One could only imagine the wide variety of inquiries that were posed to the Holy Father: challenges with the culture, difficulties in the priesthood, people not wanting to live their Faith ... The list goes on. But my buddy said that Pope Benedict's answer to every question that was asked him was the same: *Be holy.*

Holiness is the answer to all of life's questions. This is true not only in the priesthood but in all walks of life. The Second Vatican Council called this the *universal call to holiness.*[56] Being holy is not only our personal path to fulfillment and joy but also the most effective thing we can do for the entire Body of Christ and for the rest of the world as well.

I love St. Paul's analogy of the Church as the Body of Christ. It fits so well in so many ways, especially regarding holiness. Think

[56] See *Lumen Gentium*, chapter 5.

of your own body: the best thing my little toe can do for the rest of my body is to be the best little toe it can be. It needs to hold its position and not try to be a little finger. When it is operating fully as it was created to be, the rest of my body can function at its best as well.

It is no different with the spiritual body of the Church. The best thing I can do for my brother or sister right in front of me or around the world is to be holy—*fully the man God has created me to be.*

Wise was our Holy Father to preach holiness to his priests. Not only is it the most constructive means of helping others; it is also something we can achieve. Changing reality is impossible. Flourishing in my present circumstances is feasible through holiness of life.

Be holy, for I am holy is echoed throughout Scripture—most notably by our first pope, St. Peter, when he exhorts us to *be holy.*[57] But what is holiness? No doubt there are as many answers to that question as there are people. But we can say that, at its foundation, holiness is to be Godlike. *Be holy, for I am holy,*[58] says the Lord.

You and I were created in the *image and likeness of God.*[59] If the image and likeness of God is holiness, then we most mirror Him when we are holy. In reality, holiness is not just Godlikeness; it is a participation in His divine life. Not only do we become like Him; we *become* Him. Christian tradition calls this *divinization.*

We are body and soul, finite and eternal. Holiness unites these faculties into one person. Think of Christ: He was fully human and fully divine. He was *wholly* one person. God is fulfillment.

---

[57] 1 Peter 1:15.
[58] Leviticus 11:44.
[59] Genesis 1:26.

His life is *wholeness* as much as it is *holiness.* In the Trinity there is complete fulfillment. Each Divine Person—Father, Son, and Holy Spirit—is fully God and fully Himself.

The point is that *fullness* and *wholeness* in our lives are also a participation in the divine holiness that is the life of God. When we are *fully* the men and women God created us to be, we are holy. Sounds simple, and in its essence, it is. But we cannot become fully ourselves without God showing us the way.

Discipleship is the vehicle. In it, we follow Jesus, who came to save us and lead us into divine participation. Holiness is the highway we travel down. It never ends this side of Heaven, and it is full of all sorts of twists and turns, ups and downs—kind of like a bronc. When a cowboy has a seat on a bronc, it is poetry in motion. When you and I roll down the highway of holiness, life becomes a beautiful ride.

This dynamic became very real in my life midway through seminary formation. I was blessed to spend a summer with the Institute for Priestly Formation (IPF) in Omaha, Nebraska. Along with being a great gift, this experience was perfectly timed. Seminary was going well, but I had been confronting an old wound that I didn't know how to deal with in my current context. God is so good to bring these issues up. It is not to shame us but to heal us. We, however, have to have the courage to go there with Him.

For much of my youth, I was a pretty insecure kid. This is not an uncommon reality in the growing-up process. However, it really got me off track in high school. I found myself trying to be someone I wasn't, trying to wear a cool-kid hat that just didn't fit. For some reason, I thought the person I was born to be was not the person I wanted to be.

This is basically the human condition, and mankind tries to remedy it in all sorts of ways. Fortunately, my insecurities were set aside when I moved to Montana and started working full-time. All of a sudden, Bryce reappeared. I was alive again.

Working hard at the things I loved got me out of that introspective vortex and helped me to be myself. The rub was still there, though, and occasionally we'd have to duke it out. But for the most part, I was able to stay in front of my insecurities.

The beauty of seminary is that you can't hide from yourself. And that's good news because God wants you to be you. But our Lord, in His *long-looking love*, is not afraid to wound us in order to heal us. He is very happy to bring our insecurities to the forefront in order to heal them with the light of His truth.

Well, seminary was bringing my weakness to the surface. With so many gifted guys all heading in the same direction, I found myself trying to be like the other dudes, especially those who seemed to have all the right answers. It's not a bad thing to be inspired by the actions of others, insofar as it helps you to be fully yourself. But when you find yourself forcing on a hat that doesn't fit, you've crossed the line.

Stay in your lane is what my IPF summer taught me. Having the courage and the guidance to confront these limps in life has helped me to walk and run freely—and even fly. The greatest healing came through prayer. Prayer is our deepest encounter with God. It is where we can talk to Him intimately and securely as one friend talks to another.

The scene that stands out to me the most during this time of spiritual rejuvenation is at the end of John's Gospel. Peter and the boys were out fishing when they saw the Risen Jesus on the bank of the Sea of Tiberias. Rushing to Him, they found He had cooked them breakfast over a campfire. Amazed and overjoyed, they communed with their Lord.

After a bit, Jesus took Peter out for a hike and along the way He reconciled Peter's threefold denial of Him through Peter's declaration: *You know everything Lord. You know that I love You.*[60] But what struck me the most is the scene that comes next. Peter turns and sees John, the beloved disciple, following them. In envy, he says to Jesus, "Lord, what about this man?" Jesus slaps Peter upside the head and says, *Don't worry about it. I'll take care of John. As for you, follow me!*[61]

Follow me: it's the cure to all of life's insecurities. It is so easy to admire the qualities of others while degrading my own interests and worth. Following Jesus diffuses all envy and insecurities. The temptation is often to follow someone else—and, in the cases I've been describing, to follow someone who is following Jesus. To which Jesus says to us, *No, you follow me!*

How easy it can be to get out of our discipleship lane and follow someone else. We call this idolatry. Jesus says *follow me* because He *is the way, the truth, and the life. No one comes to the Father except through Him.*[62] Not through John or Bill or Suzie or whomever. Only through Jesus! He leads us back to the Father, who created us. That's where we find true security.

Really, all insecurity is misplaced identity. It is trying to find our identity in someone or something other than God. But no one and no thing other than God Himself can ever lead us to our true self. Enter Jesus. He not only leads us home but shows us how to get there. It all begins with sonship.

It is in prayer that we encounter Jesus in these depths. Through my summerlong retreat with Jesus on the banks of the Missouri River, I was able to set my true identity on the reality that *I am a beloved son of God my Father, a brother of Jesus Christ my Lord, and a*

[60] John 21:17.
[61] See John 21:21-22.
[62] John 14:6.

temple of the Holy Spirit, my Giver of life. The same truth goes for all baptized Christians.

I hit the ground running when I got back to seminary that fall. IPF taught me that the *priest God wants me to be is the man He created me to be.* It's simple. God called me off the ranch not to become someone I'm not but precisely to become *fully the man He created me to be.* The way is discipleship. If we stay in our individual lane as *beloved sons* and follow Jesus as *disciples*, He will lead us all into holiness of life.

Holiness is the life of God, and the way to get there is through the grace of God. Grace is another concept that is hard to put in a box, probably because you can't. But what we can say, as does the *Catechism of the Catholic Church*, is that "Grace is a *participation in the life of God*" (no. 1997). I am fully convinced that grace is what every human being in this world is looking for. Whether we know it or not is a different story. Grace is the Catholic Cowboy Way of life.

Grace is the means to holiness. Without grace, we could only be nice guys at best. With it, we can become saints! What I love most about grace, besides the fact that it is a participation in God's life, is that it is personal. The same grace can look completely different on me as it does on you. That's the beauty of it; grace is God's particular love dwelling in you and me.

The code to activating such liveliness is written on our hearts. St. Thomas Aquinas taught that *grace builds on nature*—meaning it works only in accordance with the particular design of the person it is acting on. Further, if you are trying to be someone God didn't create you to be, you are going to frustrate grace. It's like putting gasoline in a diesel truck; it doesn't work.

Grace fuels holiness. But the correct combination is crucial. Our deepest nature is human nature, and in that we are also *created male and female.*[63] Even though our male and female natures have some great commonalities, it is necessary to make a clear distinction for grace to be properly active in our lives. God's grace operates in unison with the DNA He encoded us with.

But grace goes beyond our genetics into the nature of our own personality. I suppose this develops as life goes on. Grace is so dynamic. It isn't a script that was written before we were born but a promise of God's continual presence in our lives. Through grace, He continues to participate in our lives, as we get to participate in His. Like a parent journeying with his child as he grows and matures, so too does God's grace meet us wherever the river of life leads us.

I love cowboying. I probably ranch harder today than ever. Starting horses and driving cattle enlivens my soul. Working on our little place back home with Dad is an oasis of grace for me. By acting in accordance with the nature and environment the Lord has planted me in, I am able to flourish into the man He created me to be.

God's grace builds on my personal nature, as it does with all of us, whatever our gig is. The Catholic Cowboy Way is discovering what our gifts and interests are and then running with them. It may be riding and roping, or it may be biking and writing. The point is to be you, authentically you. Being different isn't the point; discovering your genuine self is.

This, then, is where God's grace can transform our lives. But His grace is not magic nor instantaneous. Grace is like a glacier. It can move mountains, but it takes time. We have to be patient and persevere for God's grace to bear fruit. Grace is also not stagnant, it takes our participation to activate it. Catholic theology calls this *cooperation.*

---

[63] Genesis 1:27.

Cooperating with God's grace is like pedaling a bicycle. God gives us the bike with all its potential. But we have to climb on and work. We have to exert the energy to pump the pedals. We have to choose to get back on after we crash and burn. But when we nail it, life is a ride.

Think of Elijah in the Old Testament. The man was shot from running from his adversaries. So he sat down under a broom tree to rest. God miraculously fed him there. But that wasn't enough. He had to *get up, and eat and drink.*[64] Then he was strong enough for the rest of his journey to Mount Horeb. Just eating and drinking wasn't enough, though. He had to *get up* and cooperate with the nourishment God gave him.

Without a doubt, grace is free. That's what the word means: *free gift.* We cannot earn it. But we can do things to dispose ourselves to receive it, just as exercising my muscles allows room for them to get stronger. So, too, when we act virtuously and charitably, we create space in our hearts for God's grace to pump us up. The more we give, the more we are able to receive.

There is also tough grace that comes through the trials in life. Would that life were always roses and rainbows, but we all know differently. Life involves suffering. Jesus didn't come to do away with suffering. He came to redeem it, to give it purpose.

When we offer up our struggles in life, however big or small, in union with Christ's on the Cross, they become grace-filled. This purging and testing of our hearts is tough, but through faith, suffering can make room in our souls for a new and deeper grace-filled life.

God's grace active in our lives motivates us to holiness. It is super dynamic and is what all of mankind is searching for in life. But it builds on our individual and personal natures. We can't be

[64] See 1 Kings 19:1–8.

someone we aren't and expect to become the person we want to be. Only God, who created us, can enliven us to be fully the men and women we truly want to be. And He does so through grace, a participation in His divine life.

The beauty of holiness of life is that it brings glory to God. When we are living to our full potential as God's beloved children, the Father is happy. My favorite dismissal at the end of Mass is *Go in peace, glorifying the Lord by your life.* Living our life to the fullest through the grace of God brings glory to God.

And why wouldn't it? If I build something in the shop, and it does exactly what I designed it to, I'm a happy camper. If that's true with inanimate objects, how much more so with living beings? God is our personal Creator and Father. He wants us to operate out of our full potential. When we are *hitting on all eight,* God is pleased.

St. Irenaeus of Lyons is said to have declared, "The glory of God is man fully alive." One of my old seminary mentors used to love to quote this and remind us of this reality all the time. I believe it to be true. When we are holy, God is happy. And not only is God happy, but *we* are happy.

From this foundational truth comes all the other dimensions of holiness. Deep prayer and worship, heroic charity, and evangelization are all further imitations of Christ. But these look unique on all of us. The Holy Spirit inspires us all in personal ways. To be in tune with Him, we need to know who we are. We need to be holy.

Holiness of life is unattainable without God's grace. He is happy to give it to us; we simply need to be disposed to receive it. This takes conversion from sin and true discipleship. But it also requires us to come to the feast. We can't be fed if we don't show up for supper. If grace is the fuel to drive down the highway of holiness, then it makes sense to keep our tanks topped off.

Fight for Mass

Christianity is not complicated. One day our Lord was asked what the greatest commandment is. He replied, "You shall love the Lord your God with all your heart, and with all your soul, and with all your mind, and with all your strength."[65] Simple as that.

In other words, Jesus, God in the flesh, should be the center of our universe. We often speak of having a priority list, which I totally get. There is a hierarchy of important things in our lives, and it is helpful to prioritize them. A good man puts God at the top.

But the word *priority* is singular, not plural. God does not want to be one of many important things in our lives. He isn't even satisfied with being at the top of our priority list. He wants us all.

The only analogy I can think of to describe this is our solar system. There is a lot going on up there: stars are exploding, planets are spinning, and on earth life is happening. At the drop of a hat, this whole thing could turn into chaos. But it doesn't. Why? Because the sun is at the center of its orbit.

All matter in our sky is sustained because its existence is centered upon the sun. If Jupiter started revolving around Mars or

[65] Mark 12:30.

the moon peaced out and joined up with Saturn, we would all explode! The same is true for us. If our existence is centered on the Son, Jesus Christ, our lives will be harmonious. If they orbit around anything else, however, they will blindly spin out of control.

Jesus' call to love God with all our *heart, soul, mind, and strength* is not just a nice idea; it is a commandment! In other words, if you want to experience love, joy, peace, and happiness in the midst of the craziness that we call life, go all in with Jesus. He is God. He sustains us in existence. And better yet, He commands us to center our lives on Him so that we might not experience chaos. Life founded on Jesus is an *eternal rock.*[66]

Amen, brother! But what does that look like concretely? I don't doubt every human being who has ever lived desires such stability. Where I think we can get hung up with our Lord's commandment is in its vagueness. How do I actually make God the center of my existence and love Him with all my heart, soul, mind, and strength? By fighting for Mass.

Jesus is not a deceased ancient philosopher. He is alive and well in the Eucharist. At every Catholic Mass, our Lord's *Body, Blood, Soul, and Divinity*[67] are made present to us in the Bread of Life, the Eucharist. He has not left us hanging. Jesus promised to *be with us always, even to the end of time.*[68] The God of the universe comes to feed us at every Catholic Mass. That's worth fighting for.

The word *Mass* refers to our main form of liturgical worship as Catholics. It comes from the Latin dismissal, *Ite, missa est*, which literally means, *Go, it is sent.* The one sacrificial offering of Jesus on the Cross is *sent* to the Father through the priest, it is *sent* back

---

[66] See Isaiah 26:4.
[67] See CCC 1374.
[68] Matthew 28:20.

to us in Holy Communion, and we are then *sent* into the world as lights of Christ. Therefore, the *Catechism of the Catholic Church* rightfully calls the celebration of the Mass, and the Eucharist in particular, "the source and summit of the Christian life."

My life revolves around Jesus in the Eucharist. I am forever thankful that I've never stopped going to Mass. I remember my first Sunday on my own, waking up and thinking, "I guess it's up to me whether I want to go to Mass or not." I never even got that thought through my head when my uncle beat on my camper door and said, "Let's go to Mass." And I've never stopped.

By making Mass my priority, my life started to take shape. Probably the greatest fruit I noticed at this time was the continual conversation with Jesus that I began to have during the week. Suddenly I was talking to Him as one friend talks to another—super casually too. I'd be packing wheel bearings on a trailer and visiting with God. Jesus was becoming the center of my existence.

The biggest leap in the spiritual life that I ever experienced was going to daily Mass. In my early twenties, I was inspired to go to Mass every weekday during Lent as well as on Sundays. I remembered Mom's parents doing this, and their example inspired me to do the same. So in typical Bryce fashion, I went all in. I couldn't believe how fired up I got over this. Daily Mass was my priority, and I was happy to sacrifice for it.

Seven o'clock morning Mass at the Cathedral of St. Helena is where I could be found. Talk about peace! I know at that time I wasn't able to explain what was happening on the altar, but I could define what I was experiencing in my heart: peace and security. Watching the altar boys work in unison and Msgr. O'Neill reverently praying and preaching just drew my heart closer to God.

As much as anything, I was experiencing the eternal rock of the Church. The world was just starting to get crazy about then. The terrorist attacks of September 11 had just occurred, and you could feel the winds of chaos starting to blow. But inside the Church, while the Liturgy was going on, I was home.

Every Lent thereafter, daily Mass was my penance. It was hardly penitential, though. I loved it. Even outside of that sacred season I would sneak in a daily Mass when the opportunity arose. The peace and stability that the Mass rooted me in carried over into everyday life. Though I was still rough around the edges, I was experiencing an order to my life that only Jesus in the Eucharist could provide.

This drive for the sacramental Lord has never stopped. Even during my ranching years, I'd take Sundays off and go to Mass. And if I was going to town during the week, I'd organize the trip around a morning or noon Mass. This same reality continued all through seminary and into the priesthood. The main reason I was ordained a priest is to celebrate the Mass, and I continue to do so every day.

Making God—specifically in the Catholic Mass—my priority in life has made all the difference in the world. Life is a river, full of highs and lows, and rests and rapids. But in the boat that has Jesus in the Eucharist, we can remain calm and cool. The Catholic Cowboy Way forward is to take Jesus at His word and love God with all our *heart, soul, mind, and strength*.

Loving God with all our heart is nothing new in Sacred Scripture. It is commanded all over the Old and New Testaments. Jesus lists *our heart* at the top of His list of commands because it is at the core of our being. Our God is a jealous god.[69] He doesn't just want the majority of our heart: He wants it all. The sooner we get this one right, the better off we'll be.

---

[69]   Exodus 20:5.

It is always a temptation to center our love on things we can see and touch, such as a wife, children, parents, or work. Don't get me wrong; these things are good in and of themselves, but they aren't God. Only God can satisfy the deepest longings of our hearts. If we love God with our whole heart, then our love for the good things in life will find its proper place. We do them an injustice if we try to love others in the place of God. That is a weight they cannot carry.

But God can. We are meant to love God with all our heart. Then from this love of God, we are able to love others with the love they deserve. God is the source of love; it's who He is.[70] By loving Love, we can properly love others. Thus, our hearts find rest. As St. Augustine said, *Our hearts are restless until they rest in Thee.*[71]

Love of God is not a one-way street. He loves us *with an everlasting love.*[72] Nowhere is this more evident than in the life of Jesus. He died and rose for us out of love for us. And He continues to give us His love in the Blessed Sacrament. At Mass, or in Eucharistic Adoration, we find the fulfillment of our heart's deepest desire. The Mass is Heaven on earth. It is home. And it's worth fighting for.

Loving God with all our soul is equally important. The Latin word for *soul* is *anima*, which is basically our living force within. Our souls *animate* us. It is noteworthy that anytime we are speaking of the faculties or dimensions of the human person, we have to remember that they are intrinsically related to each other and are necessary for the makeup of the one human person. For example, the soul is deeply united with the heart. God dwells in our hearts and animates our souls, we might say.

---

[70] See 1 John 4:8.
[71] St. Augustine of Hippo, *Confessions*, bk. 1, chap. 1.
[72] Jeremiah 31:3.

The primary and ordinary way God dwells in us is through the sacraments. This especially true in Baptism, but also the Eucharist. Think of our Lord's words in John's Gospel: "Unless you eat the flesh of the Son of man and drink his blood, you have no life in you."[73] Jesus feeds our soul with His very own life through Holy Communion. Our Lord goes on to say, "He who eats my flesh and drinks my blood has eternal life."[74]

Eternal life is where it's at! We are meant to be Godlike, divinized. When we are nourished at Mass through the Eucharist, the Body and Blood of Jesus runs through our veins. Faith unlocks the door of this reality. It opens the gates of grace in our lives. Our *amen* before receiving our sacramental Lord says it all: *Yes Lord, I believe in You with all my heart, soul, mind, and strength.*

It is here that our cooperation with God's grace in the Eucharist begins take shape, or not. The Sacraments *are physical signs, instituted by Christ, to give grace.*[75] In the Blessed Sacrament, offered to us at Mass, God is there to fill our souls with His grace. In the reception of Holy Communion, we then *participate in the divine life of God.* The limiting factor, however, is us.

For sure, grace is a pure gift. How God acts in relation to each of us is up to Him. But we can do things to both prevent and aid the action of that grace. Sin is the biggest obstacle to God's grace becoming effective in our lives. Sin wounds our souls. Therefore, our reception of Jesus in the Eucharist can have little effect. The grace He gives us leaks out, so to speak.

St. Paul uses tougher language. He says to the Corinthians: "Whoever, therefore, eats the bread or drinks the cup of the

---

[73] John 6:53.
[74] John 6:54.
[75] See CCC 1131.

Lord in an unworthy manner will be guilty of profaning the body and blood of the Lord."[76] We should never take our reception of Holy Communion lightly. To say the least, sin in my life can make the grace we receive ineffective. However, receiving Holy Communion with unrepented serious sin on our soul can also be a *sacrilege*.[77]

Though we take Holy Communion seriously, we don't need to be scrupulous. As Pope Francis reminds us: "The Eucharist ... is not a prize for the perfect but a powerful medicine and nourishment for the weak."[78] We need the *power* of the Eucharist to help us avoid sin as well as live lives of grace. Therefore, the Church gives us ample opportunities to *examine ourselves*[79] to have souls ready to receive our Lord.

At the beginning of Mass is what is known as the Penitential Rite. Here we are given the opportunity not only to prepare our hearts for the mysteries we are about to enter into but also to seek God's forgiveness of our *venial sins*. Venial sins are lighter sins that *hurt* our relationship with God. In this Penitential Rite as Mass begins, God in His mercy forgives them, if we are contrite.

Mortal sins are another story. They are sins that *sever* our relationship with God. Think of a man who cheats on his wife. That doesn't just hurt their relationship; it kills it. In the context of our relationship with God, if we *knowingly* and *freely* choose to commit a *grave act*, such as adultery, we rupture our relationship with God. Our soul is cut off from its source of life.

---

[76] 1 Corinthians 11:27.
[77] See CCC 2120.
[78] Pope Francis, apostolic exhortation *Evangelii Gaudium* (January 1, 2013), 47.
[79] See 1 Corinthians 11:28.

God is merciful. And if we are truly sorry for such sins and have a firm resolve not to commit them again, He will restore us to a life of grace through the sacrament of Reconciliation, also known as Confession. Jesus came to reconcile us to the Father. He continues to do so through the ministerial priesthood, in which He is able to touch us and heal us.

The confessional is a *field hospital* for wounded soldiers. There, Jesus is able to resuscitate a repentant person through the words spoken to them by the priest. Luke's Gospel illustrates this dynamic when our Lord says to the lepers, " 'Go and show yourselves to the priests.' And as they went they were cleansed."[80] Through the sacrament of Reconciliation, Jesus is able to restore our ruptured relationship with God the Father.

If we have a mortal sin on our soul, go to Confession! And then go to Communion! God wants His love to live in us. He wants His grace to flow through our veins. He wants us to participate in His divine nature through Holy Communion. The Eucharist nourishes our souls with the bread of eternal life. May we fight to keep them pure, that the life of God may enliven us.

It's interesting that our Lord adds that we must love God with all our *mind*. In the Old Testament, we don't see this as part of the commandment to love God.[81] But I guess Jesus is God and can do what He wants. I remember the first time this hit home for me. During a homily at Mass, the priest challenged us, "Do you love God with your mind?"

Good question. I've never been much of an intellectual guy, but I knew that the mind was a faculty that God was asking me to use for His glory. We use our minds for all sorts of things; why

---

[80] Luke 17:14.
[81] Deuteronomy 6:5.

not use them to know God? I can't say what steps I took after this spiritual chiding, but over the years, I have come to appreciate knowing and loving God with my mind.

Along with Sacred Scripture I have found much profit in studying other Church teachings, most of which are found in the *Catechism of the Catholic Church.* I'm also thankful for the documents of the Second Vatican Council, which color much of my theological perspective today.

One such document on the Sacred Liturgy is *Sacrosanctum Concilium.* There the Church exhorts us to a *full, conscious, and active participation*[82] in the Liturgy. Engaging my mind in the knowledge and participation of the celebration of the Mass has skyrocketed my experience of it.

Little things, such as showing up early to quiet my mind, have helped me enter into a fuller experience of the Mass. More intentional steps, such as reading the Scripture readings before Mass, prepares me to hear God speak to me personally. But probably the most important action I've taken to help me get more out of the Liturgy is to learn why we do what we do in the Mass.

Much of the Mass is the priest's dialogue with God. The people participate in that sacred action through their responses and gestures. "Pray brethren," the priest says, "that my sacrifice and yours may be acceptable to God the almighty Father." The People of God are priests in the pews. They, too, offer their sacrifice to God through the priest at the Altar.

And what is this sacrifice? It is the one sacrifice of Jesus Christ on the Cross being *re-presented* to the Father and to us. In other words, that one event of Jesus Christ's Passion, death, and Resurrection,

---

[82] Second Vatican Council, Constitution on the Sacred Liturgy *Sacrosanctum Concilium* (December 4, 1963), no. 14.

some two thousand years ago, is being made present again. This is why we call the Mass a *memorial*. For the ancient Jews, a memorial was more than mere recollection. It was actually bringing the past back into the present.

In Catholic tradition this is known as *anamnesis*. More than simple remembrance, anamnesis cuts through the present into the eternal. Because Jesus is God, His actions in time have an eternal consequence. Therefore, the Sacred Liturgy pulls back the curtain of time and reveals eternity to us. When the Scriptures are read and the bread is broken, it is live!

This is why our *full, active, and conscious participation* is so critical. We are not mere bystanders. We are participants in the Trinitarian exchange of love, which is Heaven! This is why we don't sip coffee or twiddle our thumbs, waiting for the most boring hour of our week to be over. We enter into the mystery. We stand with attention. We kneel out of reverence. We sing in jubilation. All this we do because of the reality that Jesus Christ is continuing to save us.

I love the Mass. It's worth dying for. It's worth living for. And it's worth fighting for with all our *mind* and all our *strength*. Men are warriors. We are created to spend ourselves for a cause greater than ourselves. What greater cause could there be than the salvation and sanctification of the world?

I've seen men fight with extraordinary strength for ends that don't hold a candle next to the glory of the Mass. I remember one rainy spring when my uncle's ranch hand chained up all four wheels of his truck and mudded forty miles through the night to see a cowgirl. Human love propels us to extraordinary, and sometimes crazy, measures. Shouldn't divine love do all the more?

I've chained up more than once to make it to Mass. I love the challenge. It brings out the Catholic Cowboy in me. The Mass is the *source and summit* of my life. Is it yours? The Eucharist is the *pearl of great price.*[83] Nothing in this world can compare to the love Jesus offers us through the Holy Sacrifice of the Mass.

For those out there already fighting for Sunday Mass and looking to up your game, I suggest going to daily Mass. We pray in the Our Father, "Give us this day our daily bread."[84] Jesus is not referring to mere earthly food, but to *supersubstantial bread*, the Eucharist.[85] A daily dose of Jesus in the Eucharist will transform your life. At least it has mine.

If nothing else, the Mass is worth fighting for with all our strength just to say thanks to God. The Mass is a thanksgiving offering we are making to God the Father for the *life, death, and Resurrection* of Jesus Christ, His Son. Gratitude is the fundamental response we are to have toward God. Everything we have comes from Him. Better yet, in the Mass, He gives us everything we could ever want, *eternal life.*

Catholic Cowboys fight for love. Jesus said that the greatest commandment is to *love the Lord your God with all your heart, with all your soul, with all your mind, and with all your strength.* We take this call seriously. And we show it by fighting for Him in the Mass.

Here is where the rubber of our faith hits the road. It's easy to say that we love the Lord with our whole being, but it's harder to show it. The Catholic Cowboy Way is *to put our money where our mouth is* and fight for Mass, with an undivided heart, with a pure soul, with a fully informed mind, and with the strength of a warrior.

God asks us to make Him our priority—not one of many priorities but the center of our universe. An incarnate way of

---

[83] See Matthew 13:45–46.
[84] Matthew 6:11.
[85] See CCC 2837 for a deeper discussion on the Greek word *epiousios.*

living out this commandment is to orbit our lives around Jesus in the Eucharist. If this is the center of our existence, all other loves in life will find their proper balance, including love of our neighbor.

Compassion

I was talking with my cousin one day about the book *Wild at Heart* by John Eldredge. I was super fired up and told him we were going to start a revolution with our local men's group that was going to change the world. As always, he encouraged me, and then he said, "Yeah, the world could use more strong, compassionate men."

I got the strong part, but *compassionate* threw me for a loop. Com-passion, *with passion*. I get the word. But often in our culture, compassion is looked upon as being soft. Grandmas are good at it. Compassion is not necessarily a manly virtue. Or is it?

After our Lord was asked what the greatest commandment is, He followed it up with the second greatest commandment. Mark records Jesus stating, "The second is this, 'You shall love your neighbor as yourself.' "[86] Compassion is how we love our neighbor as ourselves. It puts us in their shoes and understands life from their perspective.

Some of the men I've admired the most are those who are rough and tough but at the drop of a hat will listen attentively to your story. They are able to put themselves aside and passionately

[86] Mark 12:31.

sympathize with what you are going through. They are not necessarily there to *fix* your problem but to *suffer with* you.

To *suffer with* is the literal meaning of the word *compassion*. Our Lord's suffering on the road to Calvary is referred to as His *Passion*, His suffering. The country boy Simon of Cyrene, who helps Jesus carry His Cross, offers a prime example of compassion.[87] Even though he was pressed into action, he still put himself aside and walked with Jesus in His struggle. He loved his neighbor as himself by *suffering with* Jesus.

I learned a tough lesson not long ago. It was super cold outside as I took off early in the morning to make my Sunday mission circuit. At a stoplight, I saw a woman walking briskly without a coat and her arms folded tightly. I thought, "That's crazy" and drove off. But farther down the road, I started to think about how I should respond. I went back and forth about turning around or going on. It was easy to justify both positions, so I just kept trucking.

But then I started to think about how cold she must have felt. And how cold I would have been walking around is subzero weather with no jacket. Then the response came easily: *Go back and give her your jacket.* Unfortunately, she was nowhere to be found. But the Lord was able to make a shift in my heart through this experience. When evaluating your moral response to a situation, ask not how *you* feel, but how *they* feel.

This perspective is a game changer. It helps us view life and others through the eyes of Christ, who is compassion embodied. Out of love for us, He not only walked in our shoes but took on our flesh. He not only suffered *with* us but suffered *for* us. Hence, compassion is what it means to imitate Christ.

---

[87] See Mark 15:21.

We can take it a step deeper, though, and *see* Christ in others. Jesus says toward the end of Matthew's Gospel, "Truly, I say to you, as you did it to one of the least of these my brethren, you did it to me."[88] When we serve others, we serve Jesus. The key to the moral life is seeing Christ in others.

While in seminary, my buddy's classmate spent a summer working with Mother Teresa's Missionaries of Charity. One day, a man was brought in off the street half dead, and the seminarian was asked to give the poor man a bath. He went to the sister in charge and said, "I'm sorry, but I just can't bring myself to do this." The sister replied to him, "That is Jesus. Go give him a bath." So the priest-to-be gave him a bath.

Far from being a way for browbeating us into doing something we don't want to do, seeing Jesus in others gives us compassion for them. It rises up true charity in us to help them in their need. It gives purpose to service. When we get the first commandment—to love God with all our being—right, the second commandment—to love our neighbor as ourselves—naturally falls into place when we see Jesus in others.

This Christian dynamic isn't true only when our brothers are suffering. It's true in all circumstances. In speaking to the Corinthians about the interconnectedness in the human body as an analogy of the Church, St. Paul says, "If one member suffers, all suffer together; if one member is honored, all rejoice together."[89] There is a certain amount of compassion due to our brothers and sisters who are rejoicing.

I'm happy for you is not an uncommon saying. It is our recognition that another's joy brings us happiness. When my friend gave

88 Matthew 25:40.
89 1 Corinthians 12:26.

birth to her first child, my heart truly rejoiced for her joy. I was happy because she was happy. This, too, is compassion. I was able to put myself in her shoes and enjoy her joy.

Compassion knows no limits. Our Lord elsewhere in Matthew's Gospel gives us the Golden Rule: *Do unto others what you would have done unto you.*[90] Pure logic. What goes around comes around. If you don't want to be treated badly, then don't treat others badly. This is a step in the right direction. But our Lord's advice goes deeper: if you want to be treated well, then treat others well.

This flies right in the face of our dog-eat-dog world. In reality, the best thing we can do for ourselves is to help others. If we don't step out into these waters, this spiritual logic of Jesus will never make sense. If we venture into this Christian life of charity, however, we will discover true happiness. Again, *a man cannot fully find himself except through a sincere gift of himself.*[91]

This is the secret of the saints. But what's cool about charity is that it's the gift that keeps on giving. Because the baptized are all members of the one Body of Christ, the Church, the love I show for you ends up returning to me. Think of our Lord's words: *love your neighbor as yourself.* This is not karma, but communion. And more specifically, Christianity calls this the Communion of Saints.

I love the Communion of Saints. It is one of the richest aspects of our Catholic Faith. At the heart of it is the understanding that there is no lone Christian. To be Christian is to be part of the Body of Christ. Sure, a body has many members, but they are in communion with one another. No member of the human body can live apart from the whole. And it's the same with Christianity. We are intrinsically united to one another.

---

[90] Matthew 7:12.
[91] Second Vatican Council, *Gaudium et Spes*, no. 24.

The beauty of this is that not even death can separate the bonds of love that unite the Body of Christ, the Church. Christian tradition has always distinguished between three aspects of the Church: the Church Triumphant, our brothers and sisters in Heaven; the Church Suffering, those members of the Body who are being purified in Purgatory on their way to Heaven; and the Church Militant, you, I, and all the members of the Body still slugging it out here on earth. Though distinct, we all remain in communion and can intercede for each other.

To intercede on another's behalf is another way of being compassionate. To be clear, as is St. Paul, "there is one mediator between God and men, the man Christ Jesus."[92] And we, as members of Christ's Body, can implore God's grace and mercy for our brothers and sisters because of our communion with Christ. I would not hesitate to pray for you if asked. Just so, our big brothers and sisters in Heaven will gladly do the same.

Scripture testifies to the power of this intercession from on high. St. James proclaims that the "prayer of a righteous man has great power in its effects."[93] Who is more righteous than those in Heaven, the Church Triumphant, who *see the face of God?*[94] Their prayers on our behalf are *like the smoke of incense from the hand of the angel before God.*[95] The Church on earth becomes stronger as more of us cross the goal into Heaven and intercede for those still in battle.

This is why I love to pray for those in Purgatory, the Church Suffering. Our prayers on their behalf help them on their journey home. Think of Judas Maccabeus, who led the Jewish revolt a

[92] 1 Timothy 2:5.
[93] James 5:16.
[94] Revelation 22:4.
[95] Revelation 8:4.

couple of hundred years before the birth of Christ. As some of his soldiers fell, he had a collection taken up and had prayers offered for them in Jerusalem. Scripture tells us that this was "a holy and pious thought. Therefore he made atonement for the dead, that they might be delivered from their sin."[96]

Scripture also testifies *that nothing unclean can enter Heaven.*[97] Therefore, the *Catechism of the Catholic Church* defines Purgatory as a place of "purification, so as to achieve the holiness necessary to enter the joy of heaven." It is experienced by those "who die in God's grace and friendship, but [are] still imperfectly purified."[98] You and I can assist in this purification process by atoning for their sin with our prayers.

Growing up, during our prayer before meals, my family always prayed that "all the souls of the faithfully departed, through the mercy of God, rest in peace." This also was a pious and compassionate action for our brethren in need. Not only do we want them to be at peace and experience the bliss of eternal life, but the more soldiers we have in Heaven interceding on our behalf, the better we'll be able to fight the good fight on earth.

For you and me, the Church Militant, life on earth is a battle between good and evil. It is foolish to go at it alone. Our enemy is too strong. We need not only the grace of God, but also the intercessions of the saints in Heaven. Think of Moses in the Old Testament: when he stood on the mountain and held his hands up, the Israelites prevailed in battle.[99] It is the same with our brothers and sisters in Heaven: when they intercede for us, we win the fight.

---

[96] 2 Maccabees 12:45.
[97] Revelation 21:27.
[98] CCC 1030.
[99] See Exodus 17:11.

The saints in Heaven show the ultimate compassion, for they truly love us as themselves, and often they do so in such human ways. Some of my favorite saints are those who are not canonized, such as my grandma, Mom's mom. Since the moment she died, I have felt very close to her, and she has given me gifts that only grandmas can give.

I can recall many such gifts, but the one that stands out the most is my hat. In the spring of 2020, I had just come off a revitalizing eight-day retreat. As I made my way *down the mountain*, back into town, I realized I needed a new hat. *No one puts new grace into an old hat.*[100] So I simply asked Grandma to help me find a hat. As I rolled through town, I remembered that the truck stop carried the kind of straw hats I like. So I swung in to see what I could find.

I tried on this one and that, but none fit. Finally, there was one with brown trim around the brim. It wasn't really my style. But as I tried it on and found that it fit, I turned and saw a truck driver in the candy-bar aisle. When our eyes met, he gave me a simple head nod and a big thumbs-up. I knew then that this was my hat, and what joy it has brought me since.

But my heavenly grandparents' intercession with my cowboy hat didn't stop there. Grandpa, Dad's dad, had died that spring. He used to say, *Always wear a hat*, to keep the sun off you. During a meeting after that retreat, as people were saying this and that and I sat there silent, I found myself taking off my hat and trying to force myself to add something to the discussion.

Later in prayer, I reflected on that, as I noticed that my heart had become heavy. I turned and saw my new hat sitting beside me in the chapel, and I recalled Grandpa's words. But this time,

---

[100] See Matthew 9:17.

instead of saying "Always wear *a* hat," he said to my heart, "Always wear *your* hat." In other words, never stop being the man God created you to be.

It can be so easy to try to be someone you're not. My little stunt in the office meeting was a prime example of that. I'm not a desk-job priest. It's not in my nature. Sure, that is part of my priestly responsibilities, but I don't have to take off my hat to do so. I can still be Bryce even when Fr. Bryce comes to call.

My grandparents continue to guide and teach me even after their death. My simple cowboy hat has a depth of meaning that all the books in the world cannot contain. Their intercession has taught me that by staying in the saddle of sonship, *always wearing my hat*, I can have peace and joy in all of life's circumstances.

I do also love the canonized saints in Heaven. These are our older brothers and sisters, or our spiritual cousins, and they love doing good for us. I think of St. Thérèse of Lisieux, who said before her death, *I will spend my Heaven doing good on earth.*[101] The saints in Heaven, whether canonized or not, spend themselves in love, by being compassionate to us in need.

So what's the difference between the Saints and our heavenly grandparents? Well, first of all, canonized saints are not in Heaven because the Church says so. All saints are in Heaven because of God's grace and their cooperation with it. The difference between all the holy men and women throughout the ages who are in Heaven, whose names we may not know, and the canonized saints is that the Church has determined that the latter are definitively there and are worthy of public veneration.

Two main criteria determine whether those who have died are to be canonized: were their lives on earth were marked by heroic

[101] St. Thérèse of Lisieux, *Story of a Soul*, epilogue.

virtue and are there substantial miracles attributed to their intercession after their death.

After Christ, there is no greater example to follow than the Saints. I think of guys like Pope St. John Paul II. I never met him, and his life was drastically different from mine. But the way he lived his life speaks to me. The stories I've heard about him and the depth of his teaching bears fruit in my life.

This is not static head knowledge, though. I've truly come to know the man. When he was alive on earth, he was just a distant figure. But since he has died and gone to Heaven, we are good friends. I can see his intercession. The way he integrated his faith into every aspect of his humanity not only inspires me but also teaches me to do the same in a culture that is very different from his.

All saints can intercede for us in miraculous ways. What's neat about those who are canonized is that they have a specialized field of compassion. They are declared *patron saints* of a particular area of life so that we can zero in on our specific needs. If you are in need of rain for your crops, ask St. Isidore the Farmer to pray for you. He's been there.

We also venerate the saints. Veneration is a way of distinguishing the honor we give the saints from the worship we give God. Adoration or worship is for God alone: Father, Son, and Holy Spirit. However, veneration, or holding in high honor those who are in communion with Him, is a rich way growing closer to God.

Through Jesus, God has revealed Himself as a human person, having a human body. A body is insignificant without its members. It's just an idea. But through the members of a body—hands, heart, head—we come to know the whole person. It is so similar with the Body of Christ, the Church. The more we know the members, the saints, the more we know the Person, Jesus.

The Church is dynamic. Her head is in Heaven while her feet remain on earth. No member of the human body lives for itself, and it should be the same with Christ's spiritual body. Love calls us to service. And in serving, we find who we are created to be.

Compassion is where love is found. It gets us out of our own little world and helps us discover the richness of the Body of Christ. It allows us to suffer with one another. It gives us vision to see Christ in everybody. Through it we can also rejoice with one another. Fundamentally, compassion is how we *love our neighbor as ourselves.*

Compassion is the virtue of the saints. We do well to follow their example and ask for their intercession. Christianity is about not going at it alone. Even Jesus had His mother and His friends who helped Him along the way. Compassion is the Catholic Cowboy Way of life. It is our Lord's second greatest commandment, but it's not His last.

8

Behold Your Mother

The final words of a dying man are significant, and it's no different with Jesus. As He hung upon the Cross He gave two final commandments, one to His Mother and the other to you and me. "When Jesus saw his mother, and the disciple whom he loved standing near, he said to his mother, 'Woman, behold, your son!' Then he said to the disciple, 'Behold, your mother!' And from that hour the disciple took her to his own home."[102]

The beloved disciple John is often seen as an image of all disciples. His intimacy with Jesus we are encouraged to foster, and we are commanded to have his love for Mary. Tradition has also held that the home that John took Mary into was his heart. She became his mother, and he became her son.

I love Mary. When it comes to the Communion of Saints, she ranks right at the top. She is not divine, but she was immaculately conceived. She was a virgin before, during, and after the birth of her Son Jesus. When her earthly life was complete, she was assumed body and soul into Heaven. And because Jesus is God, intrinsically

---

[102] John 19:26–27.

one Person with two natures, human and divine, Mary is rightly called the Mother of God.[103]

There is also the simple logic that by virtue of our Baptism, Jesus' Father has become our Father. The same is true with His Mother. Because Jesus has become our Brother, His Mother, Mary, has become our Mother as well. But have we taken our Lord's dying words seriously and invited Mary into our lives?

Fostering a devotion to Mary was probably the first extraordinary step I took into the spiritual life as a young man. I was going to Sunday Mass, but I hungered for more. I had quite a bit of windshield time on long tow truck hauls that I wanted to use to grow closer to God. So the Holy Spirit placed in my hand the Holy Rosary.

It took years to polish, but praying the Rosary has led me deeper into the mysteries of Christ. It is like putting my hand in Mary's while contemplating Jesus' life and my participation in it. Through my praying the Holy Rosary, Mary inspired me to go to daily Mass and eventually make my way to the altar of Christ as a Catholic priest.

Today, I don't leave the house without praying the Rosary. It *puts my soul at rest like a little child in its mother's arms.*[104] Devotion to Mary through the Rosary has led me intimately closer to her Son Jesus and His divine will. As the final recorded words of Mary suggest, "Do whatever he tells you."[105]

Mary's intercession for her children—you and me—is second to none. Being *full of grace,*[106] she has a mother's intuition that

---

[103] These are the four Marian dogmas of the Church. If you have a problem with Catholic veneration of Mary, please read *Jesus and the Jewish Roots of Mary* by Brant Pitre, and then let's talk.

[104] Psalm 131:2.

[105] John 2:5.

[106] Luke 1:28.

knows what her children need before they do. Such graced insight reminds me of my own mother.

When I was eighteen, I didn't know what to do with my life. But Mom did. She may not have known the full picture, but she knew that the next right step for me was to get out of Dodge.

In my last semester of high school, Mom went to her brother and asked if I could work for him. I didn't know what that entailed, but something in my heart told me to trust her. Doors opened, and two days after graduation, I moved to Helena, Montana. No other move has had such a positive impact on my life. Mom's behind-the-scenes intercession moved mountains so God's grace could abound.

It's the same with Mary. She knows what we need. Think of our Lord's first miracle. Jesus seemed pretty content being a carpenter and hanging out with His boys. Then came the hour came when, at a wedding, His Mother told Him it was time to go to work.[107] Being God, Jesus knows all things. But in His humble humanity, Jesus allowed Mary to signify the beginning of His messianic ministry. She called Him forth and the rest is history.

Moms are good at that, but so are women in general. At the beginning of time, God said *it is not good for man to be alone*.[108] So He made him a helpmate, a woman. Unfortunately, the first woman, Eve, didn't help the first man, Adam, to follow the Father's will. However, the new Eve (Mary) did help the new Adam (Jesus) fulfill the will of the Father.

I love women. They can inspire a man to do some of the dumbest things in the world. Take my favorite sport: branding. When cowboys are wrestling calves, there is a certain amount of healthy

[107] See John 2:1–11.
[108] See Genesis 2:18–23.

competition going on. Seeing my buddy Ryan have a nice throw on a calf encourages me to wrestle one even smoother. But if there's a cute cowgirl walking around, watch out! All of the sudden, dust is flying. Now it's not so much your buddy you want to outdo, but the girl you want to impress.

There is something in the feminine nature that brings out the man in men. Granted, in our fallen world, this is not always properly ordered. But the same dynamic remains. Men need a woman to fight for, to die for. For Jesus, that woman was Mary.

The Greeks called this kind of love *agape*. Agape moves beyond the passionate love of *eros* into a sacrificial love that seeks purely the good of the other. Women can bring this out in men, and I have no doubt that Mary did the same for Jesus.

Scripture tells us that at the foot of Jesus' Cross stood His Mother.[109] Chances are she was also in view as He carried His Cross up Calvary. I've often wondered why Jesus didn't just give up and die at the bottom of that hill. After all, He knew it was leading to His death anyway. Why suffer more than you have to?

Jesus is fully human and fully divine. And in God's infinite wisdom, it was necessary that He be crucified. But humanly speaking, I can only imagine how Mary's encouragement along the way gave Him strength to carry on. Women can motivate men. And when this is properly ordered to God, women can inspire men to die for love.

Mary is just as essential in our spiritual life as she was in Jesus' human life. His whole life was bookended with Mary, from start to finish. So when Jesus tells us to behold our Mother, He is basically saying, "Don't try to do it alone. Here's how I did it. Now follow

---

[109] John 19:25.

me!" Everyone needs a mother. Jesus did in His human life, and so do you and I in our spiritual life.

The beauty of mothers is that they keep us childlike. Jesus is the Son of God and doesn't need help staying in the saddle of His sonship, but you and I do. Thanks be to God, our spiritual Mother Mary is here to help. The twofold modus operandi of the Catholic Cowboy is to have fun and get the job done. There's no better way to keep our feet in these stirrups than in the arms of our Blessed Mother, Mary.

Scripture says that after the Fall, *God put enmity between the woman and Satan.* Good Scripture scholarship will agree that this woman is Mary, the mother of the Messiah, *whose heel will crush the serpent's head.*[110] *Enmity* isn't just a nice word for *distance.* It literally means they are enemies.

There is hatred between Mary and Satan. If fact, I'd hazard to say that the devil hates Mary more than he does Jesus. After all, nobody wants to admit that they were beat by a girl. In Mary there is no admixture of evil. *She is full of grace.*[111] So when we put ourselves in her arms, the devil can't reach us.

Most Christians will go so far as to tip their hat to Mary for her role in salvation history. But few take Jesus at His word and totally entrust themselves to her as little children. The Catholic Cowboy Way is to follow the example of Jesus. He was totally dependent on Mary as an infant is in his mother's womb. And He allowed her motherly encouragement to inspire Him to fulfill the Father's will. This is true devotion to Mary.

Toward the end of my summerlong spiritual formation program in Omaha, I had an interesting encounter with an angel of God.

[110] Genesis 3:15.
[111] Luke 1:28.

I went to shoot pool with some of the boys at a local pub, and a pretty-rough-looking gal put quarters on the table. The other guys wanted nothing to do with her, but I took her on.

I'm not ashamed to say that I won that game. The liquor on her breath made her a terrible shot. But when she went to leave, I said, "God bless you." She was totally taken back and said, "I have something for you." She went to her car and brought back a porcelain statue of Mary with a child in her arms.

I have to admit, I didn't think much of this encounter at the time. But later in prayer, I looked closer at the statue I was given. It wasn't very impressive. It was dirty and the head of Mary had been broken and glued back on. But the child in her arms intrigued me. He was a big lug with a full head of hair. Sure, it was meant to image Jesus. But as I let the Lord speak to me, I saw not Jesus in Mary's arms, but me.

This made perfect sense. The whole summer was geared toward being a beloved son of God the Father, like our Lord. This was an easy disposition to maintain within the confines of this retreat. However, I was heading back to school and was a bit nervous about how to stay in middle of that saddle. The Lord answered my concerns through this angel in disguise and the statue she gave me. *Behold your Mother!*

Game changer. As I headed back to seminary, I carried with me not only the statue but, more importantly, the lesson it contained. Ever since then, Mary has helped me to stay in the knowledge and experience that I am His beloved son. Even if I have fallen from this truth, Mary has always been there to help me saddle back up.

I couldn't be a priest today without Mary. Just as she was essential to Jesus in carrying out His mission, so is she to us in living out our vocations. Such a thought is in good company. I can't think of a single saint who didn't have a filial devotion to the Blessed Virgin Mary.

Take Pope St. John Paul II, whose papal motto was Totus Tuus, *totally yours*. This has deep roots going back to St. Louis de Montfort. It means more fully: *Jesus I am totally yours through Mary*. St. Teresa of Calcutta was also fond of saying, "Be all for Jesus through Mary."[112]

Early on in my spiritual journey with Mary I thought that it wasn't working because I felt as if I wasn't getting to know her. However, I was very much getting to know her Son Jesus. Years later, I reflected that this made spiritual sense. Mary's purpose is to lead us closer to Jesus.

If your devotion to Mary is helping you to experience Jesus to the exclusion of her, don't worry. It is working. Think of the servants at the wedding in Cana: once they were brought to Jesus, she faded into the background. Not that Mary no longer becomes apparent in our lives. Her presence is like the moon in the sky. She softly points us to the Son and then disappears when He arrives.

Entrusting ourselves to Mary goes further than the comfort of knowing that we are beloved sons. As with Jesus, she is here to help us fulfill the Father's will. We have a mission in life, and Mary wants to see to it that we accomplish it. As at the wedding feast at Cana, Mary says to us, "It's time to go to work."

There's no need to complicate matters; our mission begins with our vocation. Traditional Christianity has held out three major states in life that we may consider our calling or our vocation: marriage, priesthood, and consecrated life. Through this calling we are able to accomplish God's work.

The main purpose of our vocation in life is to die. Jesus models this on the Cross. Agape love is sacrificial love. Because of the

---

[112] For information on total consecration to Mary see *33 Days to Morning Glory* by Fr. Michael E. Gaitley, M.I.C.

Fall we have a selfish heart. Our vocation gets us out of ourselves and teaches us how to love God and neighbor. Far from being a constant crucifixion, our vocation in life is also how we experience · our resurrection.

To be sure, agape is not devoid of eros. Agape necessarily needs the passionate love from the other in order to live and die for the other. All vocations are ordered to this. Take marriage. The passionate love of the spouses leads them to the giving-of-self for children. As the Second Vatican Council states, *by their very nature, matrimony and conjugal love are ordered to the procreation and education of children.*[113]

Married couples not only fulfill God's mission for them by being fruitful and multiplying, but that's also where they find their happiness. Life leads to death. Eros leads to agape. The more we love, the more we are able to love. But death also leads to life. Agape leads back to eros.[114]

This reality is more visualized in the vocation to the priesthood. In the pattern of Jesus Christ the High Priest, God calls some men to continue His mission through the ministerial priesthood. St. Paul says for *husbands to love their wives as Christ did the Church and gave himself up for her.*[115] The priest of Christ gives his life up for the Church of Christ.

But it doesn't stop there. Just as Jesus' Crucifixion led to His Resurrection, so does the vocation to the priesthood lead to the lived experience of eternal life. This primarily comes through the priest's relationship with the Eucharist. The more time the priest

---

[113] *Gaudium et Spes*, no. 48.

[114] To learn more about the relationship between *eros* and *agape*, read Part I of the encyclical letter *Deus Caritas Est* by Pope Benedict XVI.

[115] Ephesians 5:25.

spends with the Risen Christ in the Eucharist, the more *his heart burns within him.*[116]

Sure, there is the agape of celibacy, but that is necessary for the eros of intimacy with the risen Lord. Through this exchange of love, the priest can minister to his bride, the Church—not as some worn-out, pent-up bachelor but as *a young stag leaping over the mountains.*[117]

All vocations are ordered to this mission of love. Consecrated life has the same thrust. A person in this state sacrifices intimacy with a physical spouse for intimacy with their spiritual spouse, who is Christ. The embodiment of this Spouse whom they then minister to is their community.

What's beautiful about our Blessed Mother's role in our missionary life is that she intercedes for us in ways we are not aware of. Again, think of the wedding at Cana. The newlyweds probably weren't even aware of all the commotion. Mary had new wine coming before they even knew they were out.

Consecrating our vocation to Mary is a sure way to keep God's grace flowing even when times get tough. Jesus entrusted His mission to her from the first moment of His existence on earth, and Mary saw Him through to the Cross and the Resurrection. When we entrust not only ourselves to her, but also our vocation, Mary makes sure we never run out of grace.

Mary can also help us discover our vocation. With so many voices and choices out there telling us what to do, we need someone to help guide us. Our Blessed Mother is here to help.

Discernment takes time. It also takes a heart and mind open to the Father's will. I often tell guys who are considering the

---

[116] See Luke 24:32.
[117] See Song of Solomon 2:8–9.

priesthood, "I don't care if you want to be a priest or not. Is God calling you to be a priest? If so, you'll discover fulfillment. If not, you'll find frustration." Our vocation in life, whatever it may be, is not about doing our will. It's about doing God's will.

The two don't have to contradict each other, though. In fact, when we discover our vocational mission in life, we discover happiness. Like all mothers, Mary wants us to be happy. But like all children, what we *think* will bring us happiness and what will *actually* bring us happiness may not be the same.

Our Blessed Mother knows the difference. If we surrender ourselves to Jesus through Mary with the confidence of children, she can help us weed through the desires of our hearts. Ultimately, she will be glad to help orchestrate events to help make our vocational discernment seamless. But for our part, we must not afraid to entrust ourselves to Mary.

The Catholic Cowboy Way is the way Jesus held out for us. He says to behold His Mother, and we take Him at His word. Mary keeps us in the saddle of sonship. She protects us from the devil, who can't reach us in her arms. And she ensures that we accomplish the Father's will through our vocation.

St. John took Mary into the home of his heart. Have we done the same? True devotion to Mary always leads us to her Son. From there her final recorded words in Sacred Scripture echo throughout the centuries: *Do whatever He tells you.*

This is when life gets fun. Every cowboy needs a woman to fight for, to die for, and most importantly, to live for. Mary was that for Jesus. She wants to be so for us too. Catholic Cowboys never ride alone. We stay nestled in the arms of our Blessed Mother Mary.

9

Ride for the Brand

Our vocation may be the beginning of our missionary life but it's not the end. We are called to glorify God with all our heart, soul, mind, and strength, which also includes our occupation. St. Paul says, "Whatever your task, work heartily, as serving the Lord and not men, knowing that from the Lord you will receive the inheritance as your reward; you are serving the Lord Christ."[118]

In a lot of ways, this is where the level of our Christianity is measured. It can be easy to practice our Faith inside the walls of the church building, but once back in the world, the real test begins. Is God our priority even in the workplace?

The Catholic Cowboy works for God, not for money. We need money to get along in life, and the *laborer deserves his wages*.[119] But I think the question we need to honestly ask ourselves is "What is the purpose of my occupation?"

There may not be a black-and-white answer. Providing for the family is a great good. But if the primary purpose of our jobs is to accumulate money, we might be on the wrong side of the fence.

---

[118] Colossians 3:23–24.
[119] Luke 10:7.

Our Lord says, "Do not lay up for yourselves treasures on earth, where moth and rust consume and where thieves break in and steal, but lay up for yourselves treasures in heaven, where neither moth nor rust consumes and where thieves do not break in and steal. For where your treasure is, there will your heart be also."[120] If we work for money, we will never be satisfied. If we work for God, we will find peace and purpose as well as be given all the monetary resources necessary to be happy and holy.

The difference has to do with our intentionality. Jesus goes on to say, "But seek first his kingdom and his righteousness, and all these things shall be yours as well."[121] If our priority in the workplace is the Kingdom of God, then all other goods will fall properly in place. If money—or anything else—takes center stage in our occupation, we will be perpetually dissatisfied.

Working for the Kingdom of God means riding for the brand. Most cowboys ride for another man's brand. A brand is the character symbol that is burned into an animal's hide to identify whom it belongs to. But a brand also distinguishes one ranch from another. When cowboys intentionally work for their outfit's brand, they are loyal. They willingly sacrifice to get the job done. The brand becomes the focal point of their mission.

This is nothing new. Riding for the brand is what our Lord modeled and taught. His entire focus was accomplishing His Father's will. Jesus said to His disciples, "My food is to do the will of him who sent me, and to accomplish his work."[122] Whether in word or deed, Jesus worked for the Kingdom of God. He rode for His Father's brand.

---

[120] Matthew 6:19–21.
[121] Matthew 6:33.
[122] John 4:34.

When a cowboy rides for the brand, he is fueled. When I worked for my uncle, I was on a mission. Practically nothing could stop me. I went to work early and often stayed late. Why? For a paycheck? No. For the brand. There was a job to get done, and I was the man to do it.

I served my uncle as I served God. My loyalty to him mirrored my loyalty to God. Far from being a slave, I took pride in my work—pride that came from a greater sense of purpose. And the joy I experienced in those years of hard work was the fruit that God was being glorified.

Riding for the Kingdom of God is how the Catholic Cowboy glorifies God in the workplace. But it doesn't stop there. Properly ordered, our occupation is a means of sanctifying the world. God wants us to use all the gifts and energy He gave us not just to glorify Him but build up His kingdom.

One rector of the seminary used to say, "Give as a gift what you have received as a gift." In other words, everything you have has been given to you for a greater purpose—mainly, the service of God and our neighbor. This is what it means to be a steward. As St. Peter says, "As each has received a gift, employ it for one another, as good stewards of God's varied grace."[123]

Stewardship is first of all acknowledging that everything in my life is a gift from God. No doubt I worked to help foster it, but in its essence, the gift came from Him. Stewardship secondly recognizes that these gifts are to be used to build up God's Kingdom and not my own kingdom.

What joy is found when one discovers that the very thing they love to do is what they are called to do! We basically don't even need to get paid because the satisfaction of providing for others'

[123] 1 Peter 4:10.

needs is payment in itself. I feel as if this dynamic is a foretaste of Heaven. There we will be serving the rest of the Body of Christ out of sheer love.

I've seen a bit of this in recent years. My ranching skills have gone full circle. These days, I run a few young cows on summer grass and then butcher them in the fall. There is so much satisfaction in cutting a steak or grinding hamburger in order to feed someone I know. I gladly work late into the night, not for money, but for love.

Grandma would say the same thing. Her meals are extraordinary. Love is her secret ingredient. But she says it's no fun to cook for one. The joy comes in feeding others. What wisdom our elders have to teach the younger generations!

Every kid graduating high school is asked the million-dollar question: "What do you want to do for the rest of your life?" That can create a lot of stress. But shifting the perspective from that to "What kind of service can you provide?" can ease the pressure. Thinking like that taps into the human heart. We are meant to provide for others. It is part of our redeemed human nature. And here's where creativity is found.

We stifle the Spirit if we simply stop at "How much money can I make?" Again, money is not inherently bad. It's the *love of money that is the root of all evils*.[124] The problem begins when the buck stops at the bank. If money is our end goal, we'll never have enough. If the Kingdom of God is our occupation's destination, we'll be happy flipping burgers for minimum wage.

I love America and the freedom that she ensures. Her very principles are founded on the flourishing of the human person and the common good of all. However, I criticize the idea Americans can have about making as much money as they can as fast as

---

[124] 1 Timothy 6:10.

they can and then retire with their feet in the sand. Such selfish ideology falls short of true freedom.

Retirement as the goal of *all our toils under the sun*[125] misses the mark. There is nothing wrong with prudently saving up money and enjoying the golden years of life. But making that the goal of one's career will ultimately not satisfy the heart.[126] It also lacks the grandeur of purpose that the human person so ardently desires.

This understanding was a big turning point in my young life. September 11 rocked the world as well as my twenty-one-year-old mind. All of the sudden, my thinking started to broaden. Is worldly pleasure really the goal of our life on earth? Are we really called to live as large as we can here and then just slip into an eternal life that's better than this one?

Such thinking never satisfied my heart. There's got to be more. Breaking the mold of such modernist thinking is what set me on course to the priesthood. It caused me to realize that if God created me, He must have a purpose for my life.

Purposeful living is the key to a fully driven life. God has a mission for our lives on earth, no matter what stage of the game we are in. The beauty of that purpose is that it participates in our goal of Heaven even now! Engaging the present moment is an opportunity not only to build up the Kingdom of God, but also to live in that reality now.

This is what it means to ride for the brand of Christ. Jesus lived every moment intentionally focused on the Kingdom of God. He saw that the fruits of His labor were meant to blossom fully in eternal life. He shot beyond this world. Such perspective gave Him not only purpose and drive but also joy.

---

[125] See Ecclesiastes 1:3.
[126] See Ecclesiastes 6:1–2.

Jesus' life was no walk in the park. *Eternal perspective* was the key to His determination. He lived the present moment from the perspective of heavenly reward.

The Letter to the Hebrews states that *for the joy that lay ahead of him, Christ endured the Cross.*[127] Humanly speaking, Jesus was able to endure such suffering and pain and not quit until all was finished because He had His sights set on Heaven. Knowing that the suffering of the Cross would lead to the joy of the Resurrection gave Him hope in His time of trial.

God brings good out of evil. That's the Gospel truth. We see it ultimately with Jesus' death and Resurrection, but no doubt we've also seen it in our own lives. Experience tells us that even the greatest tragedy can bear good fruit. *Everything happens for a reason*, as my buddy always says.

The truth is that God's will cannot be thwarted. Because He is the Creator and Sustainer of all that exists, nothing can happen outside of His will. In both His *perfect will* and *permissive will*, God always looks to our greater good. So great is our God that He is even willing to allow us to experience tragedy and trial in order for us to grow and be strengthened in faith.

Frustration occurs when we don't accept reality for what it is. We get disturbed when we wish things were different. But God's will is now, even in the midst of the *mud, and the blood, and the beer* of life. If, in faith, we can align our wills with His, trusting that He can bring good out of all situations, we can experience hope when all seems hopeless.

Our Lord modeled this way of hope for us. In the midst of His agony in the garden, before His suffering and death, Jesus struggled. *Father*, He said, *if You can, let this cup pass from me. Nevertheless, not*

---

[127] Hebrews 12:2.

my will but Thy will be done.[128] Prior to this, Jesus' *soul was sorrowful even unto death.*[129] But after conforming His will to the Father's, Jesus *rose* and faced reality.[130]

We too can *rise* and face reality with the confidence and hope of Jesus by trusting in God's providence. Nothing happens outside of the Father's will. And as a loving Dad, He intends all things for good, even our sufferings.[131] Catholic Cowboys who ride for the brand of Christ bear patiently the trials in life, knowing that God will bring good out of evil.

The beauty of a brand is that it is a physical sign of our mission, our goal, our purpose. In ranch world, it is that constant reminder that motivates us in good times and in bad. For Jesus, we might say His brand was the Cross. He always talked about it. He used it in various contexts. And it symbolized His purpose in this life.

I love brands. Growing up, we knew all about them—how to read them, whose brand was whose—and we even eventually had our own. *Lazy 6 over 6* was the family ranch's brand. It was cool and characterized who we were and what we were about. Our individual brands today continue to do the same.

Many brands for Christ have been used over the years. We see the early Christian symbol of a fish, known as the ichthys. Later the Chi-Rho symbolized Christianity. It took the first two letters of the Greek word for Christ, X and P, and melded them into one. This brand continues to identify Christians all over the world.

The brand for the Catholic Cowboy Way adds a western dimension to the Chi-Rho. We throw a quarter circle under it and call

---

[128] Matthew 26:39.
[129] Matthew 26:38.
[130] Matthew 26:46.
[131] See Romans 8:28.

it the *Rockin' Chi-Rho*. We've used this brand in all sorts of ways over the years. From youth ministry to men's retreats, the *Rockin' Chi-Rho* serves as a physical reminder to follow Christ with all our heart, soul, mind, and strength.

You can see different dimensions in the image itself. *Jesus rocks* is an obvious one. The Catholic Cowboy Way is to kick out the idea that Christianity is lame. Jesus came that *we may have life and have it to the full!*[132] Riding for the brand of Christ is the pathway to adventure, joy, and the fulfillment in life that we all desire.

Following Jesus also makes us *smile*. You can tell a tree by its fruit. A frown and Christianity are incompatible. If I'm in a prolonged period of desolation, it might be a sign that I am not traveling down my lane of discipleship. Sure, life has its ups and downs, but the wrinkles of the saints are from smiling.

One of the most beautiful smiles I've ever seen was on the face of Mother Teresa. History would be hard-pressed to present a person who rode solely for the Kingdom of God like St. Teresa of Calcutta. Her leathered face told her story. But hidden in her eyes and behind her smile was a joy that amazed the world.

The greatest image that the *Rockin' Chi-Rho* brings to the Catholic Cowboy Way of life is a question: *Am I in Jesus' boat?* It would be interesting to count how many Scripture stories involve Jesus and His disciples in a boat. It's a very common theme—and not just as an image of the past but as one that is pertinent today.

Probably the most vivid boat story of Jesus is in Matthew's Gospel:

And when he got into the boat, his disciples followed him. And behold, there arose a great storm on the sea, so that the

---

[132] John 10:10.

boat was being swamped by the waves; but he was asleep. And they went and woke him, saying, "Save, Lord; we are perishing." And he said to them, "Why are you afraid, O men of little faith?" Then he rose and rebuked the winds and the sea; and there was a great calm.[133]

Despite the chewing out of the boys for their lack of faith, this is a truly awesome scene. Riding with Jesus is an adventure that never ends. I would have been scared too if I were aboard that boat. But Jesus wasn't. In fact, He was asleep! Imagine if Jesus wasn't in their boat but they were off by themselves. They would have perished out of sheer fright!

Life is like the sea, calm one day and hectic the next. Remaining peaceful during the storms is the trick. There is truly no need to be frightened if we are disciples in Jesus' boat. Two things are certain: we will not capsize, and we will reach the other side.

But we can choose not to be in Jesus' boat, not to ride for His brand. That's when life becomes scary. Not only may we capsize and drown, but we also may not make it to the other side—Heaven. Neither is a chance I'm willing to take.

Riding in Jesus' boat is not arbitrary. He has set up His Church to be a ship that no storm can wreck. Jesus said: "And I tell you, you are Peter, and on this rock I will build my Church, and the gates of Hades shall not prevail against it."[134] When we are in full communion with the Catholic Church, we are safely in Jesus' boat.

There are so many symbols of the Church in Scripture: a body, a ship, a rock. Again, the Second Vatican Council states that the Church is "the kingdom of Christ now present in mystery."[135]

---

[133] Matthew 8:23–26.
[134] Matthew 16:18.
[135] *Lumen Gentium*, no. 3.

We don't need to look to the heavens to discover the Kingdom of God. The Kingdom is *already present* to us on earth through the Catholic Church, with Peter at the helm.

"Am I in Jesus' boat?" is a worthy gut check at all times in our life. If not, good luck. If so, be at peace. No storm can crash this traveling Kingdom of God. The *Rockin' Chi-Rho* is a visible reminder of our communion with Christ and His Church. When we ride for this brand, life is fun, and we get the job done.

The truth is, if we have been baptized, we have been branded for Christ. Baptism places an indelible mark on our souls. We are God's. We are part of His herd. So we might as well ride for it.

There is pride in this reality. Jesus has saved me and claimed me for His own. I'm part of the herd, and I'm also co-owner of the ranch. When I left ranching and went to seminary, one motivating thought was "I'll have my ranch in Heaven." In other words, my ranching passion will be somehow satisfied in Heaven, and better than I can ever imagine.

The Kingdom of God fulfills all our human desires. We catch a glimpse of it on earth, but only in eternal life will our hearts fully find rest. *Eye has not seen, ear has not heard, nor has it dawned on the mind of man what God has in store for those who love Him.*[136] The good news is that we don't have to wait until death to experience Heaven. We can live already in God's Kingdom by riding for the brand of Christ.

The Catholic Cowboy Way is to *seek first the Kingdom of God and His righteousness.* We concretely do so by working for God and not for money; by using the gifts He has given us to serve Him and our neighbor; and ultimately, by conforming our wills to His, trusting that He can and will bring good out of evil.

---

[136] 1 Corinthians 2:9.

Brands are beautiful. And there is no better brand to ride for than the one placed on our hearts, the brand of Jesus Christ. Such vision gives focus to our mission. Such purpose gives joy to our life. And such drive accomplishes the Father's will. Catholic Cowboys ride for the Kingdom of God.

10

The Church Needs More Cowboys

Cowboys aren't born. They're discovered. I'm fully convinced that the cowboy spirit lies deep within all of us. Some may ride and rope for a living, while others may never step foot on a working ranch. Either way, the world is longing for more cowboys. And not only the world: the Church needs more cowboys too.

One of my favorite country songs is "The World Needs More Cowboys" by Chancey Williams. In it he sings: "They come in every size and color, hell from all over this world. Some of the toughest cowboys I ever met were cowgirls."[137] So true. There is no one-size-fits-all cowboy hat. The whole purpose of the cowboy way is to be authentically you—male or female; black, white, or whatever.

When guys ride with me, I outfit them with a new straw hat. I suppose it's part of the father in me. But the deeper meaning is found in my granddad's lasting words: *always wear your hat*. Be yourself, and you'll become who God created you to be.

Our Lord hated hypocrisy, and so does everyone else. But we are tempted by it daily. Always in front of us is the façade the world wants

---

[137] Chancey Williams & the Younger Brothers Band, "The World Needs More Cowboys," *3rd Street*, Younger Brother Records, 2020.

us to wear. *Dress like this. Say this stupid thing. Act immorally. Blah blah blah* ... In other words, be anyone but who God has created you to be.

No thanks. The Catholic Cowboy Way is one of genuineness. The path to true freedom lies in authenticity. This is where life starts, but it doesn't end there. Jesus is the *Alpha and Omega, the beginning and the end.*[138] He *is the way, the truth, and the life.*[139] In following Him, we find ourselves.

Cowboy Catholicism is a spirit. Sure, the hat embodies it, but it doesn't define it. What defines the Catholic Cowboy is holiness, *being fully the person God created you to be.* That may or may not entail breaking horses and butchering beef. But these same virtues are translatable into all walks of life.

Of all the virtues that the cowboy embodies, I'd say courage stands out the most. One fall, we had a wild bunch of horses across the river, and they wouldn't come home. Gathering up a posse of riders, we set out to bring them back. It would not be an easy task. My horse had already been dumped in the water on a previous attempt. I was scared.

As we saddled up and headed out, I was reminded of the saying of John Wayne: *Courage is being scared to death and saddling up anyway.* Spot on. Courage is not an absence of fear. It is bravery in the face of fear. Our mission that day was unsuccessful, but my courage was strengthened by facing my fears.

I hate fear. No doubt it has a purpose. If a grizzly is chasing you down, fear fuels you to turn and run or stop and fight. Or if you find yourself in a stupid situation and right reason suggests you should not proceed, fear can rightly cower you. Aside from that, fear has little place in the Christian life.

---

[138] Revelation 22:13.
[139] John 14:6.

Our Lord said over and over again to *be not afraid.*[140] His insistence on this highlights two things. First, fear is a real component in our lives. Second, *perfect love casts out all fear.*[141] Truth and love are the antidotes to fear.

Knowledge is powerful. Understanding how the human person works is key to the proper operation of ourselves. Fear is an emotion. It is an instinctual device that causes us to react. If a grizzly is running you down, don't think. Act.

That being said, fear gets more credit than it is due. That's why our Lord commanded us not to be afraid. If left unchecked, when fear arises the heart and mind blindly follow. But emotions are not meant to do our thinking. Reason is. Properly ordered, emotions inform the intellect, and then right reason makes a decision.

All too often, though, emotions arise, and we follow. This disorder can have all sorts of negative implications in life. Think of an unruly horse. If emotions do our thinking for us, we are like a rider on a runaway colt. If right reason tempers our emotions, though, horse and rider trot along in harmony. Emotions are neutral, neither good nor bad in and of themselves. It's what we do with them that matters.

When reason judges that this or that emotion derives from good roots, then accept it and proceed as follows. When reason judges that a particular emotion is based on incomplete facts and will lead to negative consequences, proceed with caution, to say the least.

This is even truer when it comes to fear. If fear does our thinking for us, we are doomed to a life of anxiety and cowardice. If fear is checked by right reason, we can live a life of prudence and courage.

[140] See Luke 5:10, for example.
[141] 1 John 4:18.

One way of discerning the accuracy of our emotions is with the backdrop of truth. Does this fear measure up to the facts of reality? According to my calculation of the data, consistently across America during the Covid-19 pandemic, 99 percent of people who contracted the virus survived it. Yet millions of people viewed it as a death sentence. Who was driving that bus—fear or reason?

The devil is happy to sell us partial truths. There is truth that Covid-19 is a deadly virus. But is that the complete picture? The fullness of the truth also takes into account that roughly 1 percent of the people who get the virus actually die from it. The odds of survival are pretty good, I'd say. The point is, don't let fear rule your life. Test it with the fullness of truth.

Jesus says that *the truth will set you free.*[142] Our Lord came that *we may have life and have it to the full,*[143] not walk around in fear. Two of the words I hate the most in life are *what if.* If these two words are rolling around in your head, you are likely listening to fear.

What if ... Fear of the future. The most crippling words we can listen to. Again, balance that scenario with right reason. If the logical consequence of jumping off a cliff is broken legs or death, don't jump! But if I'm just scared of the future because it's unknown, so what? No one knows the future except God our Father, and He loves us.

Perfect love casts out all fear, says St. John. Why? Because fear and love are incompatible. Perfect love is the lived knowledge that God is my Father, who is in control of all forces, both natural and supernatural. Even if something truly bad happens to me, faith tells me that God will bring good out of it in the long run. Even if death is looming, I still have the hope of Heaven.

---

[142] John 8:32.
[143] John 10:10.

The father of lies, the devil,[144] is happy to tell us different. He wants to lead us into despair, fear's ultimate destination. In reality, though, the devil is a bully. He acts mean and tough, but if we stand up to his lies with the truth of God's love, he cowers. As St. James says, "Submit yourselves therefore to God. Resist the devil and he will flee from you."[145]

As with a bully, though, if we don't stand up against his tactics, the devil is no opponent to tangle with. St. Ignatius of Loyola says, "There is no beast so wild on the face of the earth as the enemy of human nature in following out his damnable intention with so great malice."[146]

There is no doubt the devil is scary, and can lead us to Hell. But that doesn't mean we have to be afraid. Catholic Cowboys already *live in the glorious freedom of the children of God.*[147] We do so by testing our fears against the backdrop of truth and in light of God's love for us. Courage is not an absence of fear but bravery in the face of our fears.

The Catholic Cowboy also walks through life with confidence. The word *confidence* derives from the Latin words *con fidere,* which literally means *with faith* or *trust.* Understanding the objective meaning in the word can help us grow in the subjective application of the virtue.

Confidence isn't just a personality trait that some are born with and others are not. It is based on truth and reality. Authentic confidence is open to all and is for all. And one of the surest ways to obtain it is by following the Catholic Cowboy Way.

---

[144] John 8:44.
[145] James 4:7.
[146] Discernment of Spirits, rule 12.
[147] Romans 8:21.

Christian confidence is based on the truth of sonship. I am a beloved son of God my father. This is my identity. This is the bedrock of every Christian. Nothing can undermine this truth, nor can anything else substitute for this foundational reality.

There is a great temptation to base our identity on other people's opinions of us. This can work here and there but not when the going gets tough. Sonship is a rock. Nothing can shake us in life if our experience of ourselves is seen in light of the Father's love for me personally. Such knowledge allows the Christian to walk through life in confidence, *with faith*, in our baptismal identity.

True confidence also comes from *trust*. St. Paul had this cowboy confidence. He would say of himself, *I can do all things in Christ, who strengthens me.*[148] One of my favorite modern devotions is to Jesus' Divine Mercy. In the painting of Him with rays representing blood and water pouring forth from His side are the words "Jesus, I trust in You."

Confidence isn't fancy thinking. It is trusting in the truth that Jesus strengthens us at all times through His grace and mercy. What I love about the Divine Mercy image is that Jesus looks to be walking backward into the unknown. And He is simply saying, "Trust me."

Such confidence (or lack thereof) reminds me of Peter walking on the water toward Jesus. When Peter sees Jesus walking on the water, he has the confidence to walk on water himself. But as soon as he takes his eyes off our Lord, he starts to sink.[149]

Trusting in God is putting our faith into action right here, right now. It gives us confidence to walk on the water of life. The converse is true too. If we start to worry about the future or dwell

---

[148] Philippians 4:13.
[149] See Matthew 14:22–33.

on the past, we start to panic and sink. Trust in Jesus gives His disciples the confidence to do anything.

Courage and confidence are two virtues that characterize the Catholic Cowboy. We all desire these virtues in our lives, but I believe God also wants them in His Church. He wants more authentic men and women of courage who seek the truth; more sons and daughters with a bold determination that won't quit until the Father's will is accomplished; more Catholics who are proud to call themselves Christian.

Truth is objective. It is black and white. The problem is that we live in a gray world. Discovering the truth is not always easy. It often takes other people's perspective to help us sift through the falsities. This is what authentic dialogue is all about: reaching the truth.

However, we can fall into the trap of thinking that truth is just a matter of opinion, therefore, relativizing it. This makes our already gray world even murkier. It also creates hostility among people of varying perspectives. Clarity in life is found in seeking the truth, not in pushing one's ideology.

Truth seeking is not solely up to man. God has established His Church to help guide us in the ways of truth. The Church speaks clearly on matters of faith and morals. Not only does this guidance help us find our truest self; it also helps us discover Truth Himself.

Jesus Christ said that He is *the way, the truth, and the life.*[150] Truth is a person. It is the second Person of the Trinity. Truth is the *Word made flesh.*[151] Seeking the Truth is the greatest exploration one can venture out on, and on it we discover the destination of life's journey, God.

The Church needs more cowboys who sincerely seek the truth. Believe it or not, such an endeavor takes courage. Truth can challenge

[150] John 14:6.
[151] John 1:14.

us to change. But it can also free us to fly. To seek truth alone, though, is a misguided journey. We need other truth seekers' perspectives to help us hit our target. Together, we can muddle through the gray of life and bring fuller color to the world.

The Church also needs more cowboys with a *don't-give-up* toughness. Perseverance and determination run deep in the Catholic Cowboy Way of life. For centuries, men and women of faith have shed their blood in witness to their love of Christ. These martyrs willing sacrificed themselves to accomplish their mission, the Father's will.

I'm not the best roper in the branding pen, so I take what I can get. One day, I came in hot with a loop around only one back leg of a calf instead of both. The young boys tried and tried but couldn't wrestle it to the ground. So they gave up! I couldn't believe what I saw. I thought, "Where have all the cowboys gone?"

Cowboys don't quit. They die. Jesus Himself is the original cowboy. *Quitting* was not in His vocabulary. One has only to meditate upon the Sorrowful Mysteries of the Rosary and walk through our Lord's Passion to taste His perseverance and determination. I think also of Him staying back in the Temple as a young boy. When His parents found Him, He simply said, *Did you not know I must be about my Father's business?*[152]

I remember one time when Dad sent us boys on a mission to move some cattle. I was pretty young, but my brothers and cousin where all older. We ventured out, and all my horse wanted to do was go home. Eventually I caved and went back to the cabin. One by one, the other riders trickled back in too.

But not Luke. He didn't show back up. I remember being worried and thinking the worst. I imagined him rolling down

---

[152] Luke 2:49, Douay-Rheims.

the canyon wall and being in trouble. But Dad said to wait. That afternoon, Luke returned. He completed the mission when the rest of us had bailed. That's cowboy tough. That's no quit.

Catholic Cowboys would rather die than abandon ship. There is pride in riding for Christ. There is purpose in fulfilling the Father's will, even if that requires martyrdom, shedding our blood for love of Christ. The word *martyr* means *witness*. Would that in the Church today there were a few more martyrs: people who witness to their love of Christ by their lives.

But what I like most about all this perseverance stuff is that it's fun. I get plumb fired up when I think about giving my all for the Father. We're all going to die anyway. Might as well *set our face like flint*[153] now and die accomplishing the Father's will rather than quitting and taking the easy route.

Country music speaks to my soul. Tim McGraw, in his song "The Cowboy in Me," sings: "We ride, never worry about the fall. I guess that's just the cowboy in us all."[154] If you're thinking about getting bucked off as you climb over the chute, you will get dumped, guaranteed. But if you're focused on the ride as you swing in the saddle, then you'll more likely have a seat.

This cowboy logic puts both courage and confidence into action. Whatever our circumstances in life are, there can always be a bad outcome. If that is our focus, we basically dupe ourselves. The mind is so powerful. If we think negative, we will likely reap negative results. If we choose a positive outlook, then we have hope.

---

[153] See Isaiah 50:7; Luke 9:51.
[154] Tim McGraw, vocalist, "The Cowboy in Me," written by Jeffrey Steele, Al Anderson, and Craig Wiseman, *Set This Circus Down*, Curb Records, 2001.

I like to say that *if you go into battle thinking you are going to lose, you will lose. If you go into battle believing you will win, then you've got a fighting chance.* The way we think affects not only the way we feel; it also affects our outcomes in life. Mental toughness is key to the Catholic Cowboy Way of life.

I was heading to the shop one day in high school, and Mr. Reachard said, "Let me see your work order," which listed what you were going to do that day. I had written, "I'm going to *try* to mount some driving lights on my bumper." He looked at me and said, "No. You're *going* to mount some driving lights on your bumper."

Try is the first step toward failure. It is thinking about the fall as you mount up. Sure, we might not succeed, but why not give ourselves a *fighting chance?* Whether you are interviewing for a job or climbing on a bronc at the county fair, don't try—do! You'll be a winner even if you lose.

The greatest bronc in the world to get the reins on is our mind. We bit that horse; we gain control of the world. There is a cowboy in all of us, and it starts with mental discipline. If negative thoughts are in the driver's seat, we're in trouble. If reasoned positive thinking has the helm, we can remain calm and cool even amid the greatest storms in life.

The Church needs cowboys even more than the world does. She needs more courageous and confident men and women, who seek the truth, who don't give up, and who are proud to be Catholic. Above all though, she needs more authenticity and less hypocrisy.

Be fully yourself is the Catholic Cowboy Way. But to become yourself, you have to find yourself. Jesus Christ is the *way, the truth, and the life.* Without Him, we will be spinning our wheels for a long time. With Him, we sit tall in the saddle of life and hold our head up high in faith.

11

On to the Next One

One of the biggest lessons in humility I ever received was getting bucked off in front of the hometown crowd at the Fourth of July rodeo. That was a long walk back to my cowboy hat. There's two ways a man can go in a scenario like that: regret the past or simply move *on to the next one*.

On to the next one is the old rodeo saying. Sure, you drove two hundred miles and paid seventy-five dollars just to get dumped in front of a grandstand of people. Now let's turn around and do it all over again. If you don't choose to move forward in adversity, the past will eat you alive.

Live and learn is the secret to regret-free living. The past can be our teacher if we let it. Or it can be a black cloud of regret that will never let the sun of hope shine through. The choice is ours, which doesn't make it necessarily easy. But God is here to help us move forward if we're open.

Three words that I am convinced never come from God are *should've*, *would've*, and *could've*. It's often true that things might be better now if things were done differently before. But the most frustrating thing in the world is to try to change the past. God is now. And the more we accept the past in light of the present, the more we can find hope for the future.

When Grandpa was teaching us kids to drive, he would always say, "Only back up as far as you need to." Words of wisdom. Most minor vehicle accidents happen in reverse. You think you are seeing clearly as you back up, but there are always blind spots. Reverse is good, to the degree that it helps you drive forward.

Only back up as far as you need to. I rarely put a car in reverse today without thinking of that. But this advice also profits us in the spiritual life. The spiritual life is about moving forward, progressing toward God. It is good to back up and reflect on past experiences, insofar as they are geared to inform the future. They can teach us what works in life and what doesn't.

But the past can also be a ball and chain, enslaving us to a life of *should've, would've, could've.* St. Paul recognized this tendency when he said, "But one thing I do, forgetting what lies behind and straining forward to what lies ahead, I press on toward the goal for the prize of the upward call of God in Christ Jesus."[155] Paul consented in the murdering of Christians before his conversion. Did he have something to be regretful for? Yes. Was he? No.

St. Paul was *on to the next one* because of our Lord's mercy toward him. God's mercy is boundless. There is no sin so great that cannot be forgiven. The only unforgivable sin is refusing to repent because we've closed ourselves to God's mercy.[156]

Think of the two thieves who were crucified with Christ. Both were guilty. But only one was open to God's mercy. Jesus said to him, "Truly, I say to you, today you will be with me in Paradise."[157]

---

[155] Philippians 3:13–14.
[156] See CCC 1864.
[157] Luke 23:43.

The same forgiveness was available to the other thief, but he was not open to it. God condemns no one to Hell. We choose Hell through unrepentance.

Being *on to the next one* doesn't gloss over the past but brings the past into the light of God's mercy and love. Jesus came to heal us. As He said, "I came not to call the righteous, but sinners."[158] And our Lord isn't just content in calling sinners. He wants to heal us too.

Bringing our wounds into the healing light of Christ is not only medicinal but also empowering. The Cross represents God's triumph over evil. Through Jesus, God can bring good out of evil. The greatest evil ever done in the world — the Crucifixion of God — brought about the greatest good ever imagined: the Resurrection of Life from the dead.

The same dynamic is open to us through the grace and mercy of Jesus Christ. St. Paul ended up boldly proclaiming his persecution of Christians because it led him to encounter the saving grace of Christ. Such grace empowered him to become arguably the greatest evangelist ever.

Encountering the healing touch of Jesus, like St. Paul or the repentant thief, is still available to us today. The sacrament of Reconciliation is a real encounter with the grace and mercy of Jesus Christ. Through true contrition, we can receive His healing mercy. Through the grace of the sacrament, we can be strengthened to *go and sin no more.*[159]

Countless saints throughout history became great heralds of God's mercy because of the mercy they received. Our Lord's bold command "Love your enemies and pray for those who persecute

---

[158] Mark 2:17.
[159] John 8:11.

you"[160] was no longer a chore for them. They naturally forgave because they had been forgiven.

Sometimes our interior wounds come not from our sins but from the sins of others inflicted upon us. A traumatic childhood or a broken marriage can leave deep wounds on our hearts. But the grace and mercy of our Lord are here to heal these wounds, no matter how big or small.[161]

Forgiveness is the greatest liberator in the world. And there is no greater gift we can give ourselves than to forgive others. Forgiveness frees our hearts. The resentment that comes from the wounds others have inflicted upon us enslaves our hearts. Forgiveness sets us free to live and love again.

Peter asked Jesus how many times he should forgive his brother, and Jesus replied, "Seventy times seven."[162] In other words, there will be countless times when people will offend you and endless opportunity for you to forgive them.

Over the years, I have boiled the processes of finding freedom through forgiveness down to three steps. Sure, every situation is unique. Some are more personal than others. And some wounds are deeper than others. But I am convinced that in time Jesus can set our hearts free through this threefold mode of forgiveness.

The first step is just to say the words *I forgive.* Jesus really doesn't give us any option. He simply says, "Forgive, and you will be forgiven."[163] But He also says, *if you do not forgive others, neither will the Father forgive you.*[164] Forgiveness is first an act of the will. It

---

[160] Matthew 5:44.
[161] For a deeper guide on healing our personal wounds, see the work of Dr. Bob Schuchts, particularly his book *Be Healed.*
[162] Matthew 18:22.
[163] Luke 6:37.
[164] Matthew 6:15

is a choice, a decision. As hard as it may be, the sooner we spit the words out, the less chance resentment has to take root.

St. Paul says that *if you are angry, let it be without sin. The sun must not go down on your wrath; do not give the devil a chance to work on you.*[165] The longer we allow the wounds inflicted upon us to fester, the deeper the roots of resentment will grow. Saying *I forgive* before we hit the hay prevents evil from doing its dirty work as we sleep.

As good as this step may be, it does not complete the picture. Jesus also says, *Forgive your brother from your heart.*[166] This is a tall order, which I'm not sure can be done without God's help. The boys were often perplexed at how high Jesus raised the bar. But our Lord never backs down. He just says: "With God all things are possible."[167]

Finding freedom of heart through forgiveness is possible only with God's grace. Therefore, do not be afraid to *ask for help.* This second step in forgiving from the heart is not to be underestimated. God wants to help us. Our Father *promises to give us whatever we ask for in the name of Jesus.*[168]

The most concrete way I've found to ask our Lord to help us forgive as He forgives is in the confessional. The sacrament of Reconciliation is a healing sacrament. Sin wounds us, whether it is our own sins or the sins of others have inflicted upon us. When we bring those wounds out of the darkness and into the light of Christ, He can begin to heal us.

I always bring my *sins* and my *struggles* to Jesus through the priest in the confessional because our Lord can not only *heal*; He can

---

[165] See Ephesians 4:26-27.
[166] See Matthew 18:35.
[167] Matthew 19:26.
[168] John 16:23.

also *help*. The beauty of Confession is that it offers us both Christ's mercy, which heals, and His grace, which helps. Jesus is here to help always. Though the sacrament of Reconciliation is not the only way Jesus can help us forgive, it certainly does aid in those big issues.

The final step in setting our hearts free through forgiving others is to *pray for them*. As our Lord says, *love your enemies and pray for those who persecute you.* Such an act demonstrates a high degree of charity, which sets Christians apart from the rest of the world.

Look at our Lord on the Cross. He says, "Father, forgive them; for they know not what they do."[169] He is praying for those who are persecuting Him. This third step of forgiveness diffuses all malice in our minds. Praying for those who have wounded us releases the claws of resentment and regret.

This kind of prayer of forgiveness is not simply asking the Lord to help heal the situation. Praying for those who persecute us comes from the vantage point of the Cross. It is entering into the compassion of Christ, who sympathized with His enemies, for *they knew not what they did*. Praying for our persecutors gets us off the *eye-to-eye* level of life and allows us to see the world from God's perspective, the perspective of charity.

From there, we look at our persecutors as brothers and sisters. Prayer like Christ's on the Cross simply asks God to bless our neighbor. How easy it is to get caught up in fantasy and let our minds fill in the gaps with information we don't know. God knows the full picture. He knows the hidden circumstances that we don't. Therefore, we simply ask God to bless our persecutors with all the virtues necessary to be *healthy, happy, and holy*.

Freedom from the sins others have inflicted upon us is possible through the process of forgiveness. It begins with the will; say the

---

[169] Luke 23:34.

words *I forgive,* even if you don't want to. Second, *ask our Lord for help.* His grace is there to aid. Finally, *pray for those who persecute you.* Then your heart will be free to fly once again.

To be fully *on to the next one,* though, we also need to forgive ourselves. Our Lord came not to condemn us but to set us free. Think of the woman caught in adultery. Jesus does not upbraid her. He simply says, "Neither do I condemn you; go, and do not sin again."[170] If Jesus doesn't condemn us, we should probably not condemn ourselves.

Easier said than done, I know. Our minds like to hang on to the past, and the devil is happy to remind us of our failings. The trick to forgiving ourselves lies in tuning out those condemning voices and tuning in to the One who sets us free.

Throughout the New Testament, the devil is revealed to us as the accuser. And the book of Revelation testifies that he *accuses us day and night.*[171] The devil is happy to rub our faces in the mud of past experiences, if we let him. But to ignore him, we need to name him.

If we name it, we can claim it. When the devil addresses us, it almost always begins with *you. You* did this. *You* weren't that. *You* should've ... *You* would've ... *You* could've ... Every accusation the devil brings before us comes from outside ourselves and usually begins with *you.*

God does not address us as *you.* This is the enemy of our human nature accusing us, and oh, how often we buy it! The devil speaks in partial truths. Is there truth in the reality of my past sins? Sure. Has Jesus condemned me? No. Therefore, shut up, loser; I'm *on to the next one.*

---

[170] John 8:11.
[171] Revelation 12:10.

We are also pretty good at accusing ourselves. Such accusations begin with *I*. *I* did ... *I* didn't ... *I* should've, *I* would've, *I* could've ... The list goes on. This is negative self-talk to it finest degree. Who is speaking here—God or I? That is our self talking, so be very careful about listening to any accusation that begins with *I*.

God calls us by name. He addresses each of us as His son or daughter. This is the voice to tune in to, but to do so, we must tune out of the *yous* and *Is*. God's voice comes from the heart; it wells up from within. Even if He does bring up past sins in order to heal them, He does so in a gentlemanly manner.

God is our Advocate, not our accuser. He does not condemn us but forgives us. We would do well to do the same to others, including ourselves. We live and we learn. There is a lesson in past mistakes that helps inform the future. Jesus tells all who are repentant, *Go and sin no more*. Through forgiveness, the past becomes a testimony to God's healing grace and mercy.

Forgiveness frees us to be *on to the next one*, but we don't want to get too far ahead of ourselves. Just as it's not healthy to back up more than we need to, so it can be detrimental to look too far ahead. Peace is found in the present moment.

The secret to bronc riding is to *keep your mind in the middle*. If you criticize your last buck for not spurring correctly, you'll lose focus on the current opportunity to spur the buck you're in. If, three seconds into the ride, your mind is dreaming about how that buckle will look on your belt, you'll likely not make eight.

Keep your mind in the middle, one buck at a time. This world will dump us if we get too far behind or too far in front of ourselves. Living in the present moment is how we keep a seat on this bronc called life.

God is now. He's not in the past, and He's not in the future. He can be in both insofar as those tenses are properly brought into the present. We learn from the past, and we also anticipate the future. *Plan your work and work your plan* is what my old man always taught me. But I do so from the now.

This is not so hard in normal circumstances. When the storms of life start to rear on the horizon, though, we can lose our focus. No need to fear: gratitude is here. I have found no better way to *keep my mind in the middle* of life than through gratitude.

In reality, man's only response to God is that of thanksgiving. In the Mass, the priest says, "Let us give thanks to the Lord our God." And the people reply, "It is right and just." To give thanks always is truly *right and just.* The very heart of the Mass, the Eucharist, is a thanksgiving offering.

St. Paul says, "Rejoice always, pray constantly, give thanks in all circumstances; for this is the will of God in Christ Jesus for you."[172] I often like to think of God's will not so much in front of us, telling us which way to go, or behind us criticizing us when we chose poorly, but being beside us, encouraging and inspiring us always. *Giving thanks in all circumstances* allows us to encounter God in the present moment of life and trust that He is with us through thick and thin.

Life is a gift. A wise priest in seminary once told me, "Gratitude is like going through life with open hands, freely receiving and freely giving." That image has always stuck with me. All too often, our hands can be closed and miss the gift of the moment the Lord wants to give us, or they can be clinging to something when God is calling us to be *on to the next one.*

This made all the more sense to me when my bike was stolen while in seminary. My spiritual director at the time simply said, "If you focus on the loss, there is sorrow. If you focus on the gift

---

[172] 1 Thessalonians 5:16–18.

the the bike was while you had it, there is gratitude." Tough, but true. Nothing happens outside of God's will. Gratitude allows us to receive the *good, the bad, and the ugly* moments in life as gifts from God.

Gratitude keeps our minds in the middle of life. It is a consistent encounter with God, who is the Eternal Now. Being intentionally thankful helps us realize that God is beside us and will provide for us in all circumstances. Thankfulness dispels anxiety and ushers in the peacefulness of the present moment.

Being *on to the next one* is the secret to the Catholic Cowboy Way of life. The first step lies in receiving God's mercy for our sinful actions. There is no better way to do so than in the sacrament of Reconciliation. Once we have received God's mercy, we are more able to forgive others, including ourselves.

With little doubt, forgiveness is the greatest prescription for all of life's woes. It frees us from the chains of resentment and regret that come from our sins and the sins of others. Above all, forgiveness makes us Christlike. Christ calls us all to *love our enemies and pray for those who persecute us,* and He models such mercy on the Cross.

Cowboy Catholicism is a tall order. It takes humility, but it also takes wisdom, which comes from *living and learning.* We move forward in freedom not just so we can make it to Heaven one day but so that we can live in that reality even now!

12

Go Fishing

I ran into my cousin one day who farms full-time, and I asked him what he had been up to. "Fishing for sauger," he said. This doesn't sound too earth-shattering, but the normal response to someone in his position would be either *just working* or *super busy*. But not Clint. He was fishing.

Part of the beauty of sonship is that the weight of the world does not weigh on our shoulders. Sure, we have responsibilities and a mission in life to carry out. But that stems from the reality that we are first sons of the Father. If it doesn't, our lives get crazy and we get stressed out.

The Catholic Cowboy Way is to take time to *go fishing*. The world will gladly eat us up and spit us out if we let it. Spending time in our personal *fishing hole* is rejuvenating. It is a genuine encounter with God, and it gives us a new perspective on life.

I am not much of an actual fisherman, so my favorite *fishing spot* is the ranch back home. Working with Dad and visiting with Mom grounds me in the reality of the Father's love. Everyone has a spiritual *fishing hole*. But do we take time to go there?

True recreation is just that: it *re-creates* us. It revitalizes us with the vigor that comes from knowing we are God's beloved sons or daughters. The world wants us to think that we are just cogs in the wheel of humanity. But when I spend time doing the things that I naturally love, I am refreshed and able take on my vocation in life with new zeal.

But even good things can be taken out of proportion. We can spend *too much* time fishing—time that should be spent with family or on other responsibilities. Authentic recreation is ordered to mission. It seeks out a genuine encounter with the source of life in order to carry out our missions in life. Without such intentionality, recreation is reduced to mere child's play.

One word that is foreign to our American vocabulary is *leisure*. On the surface, one might think of it as free time or time away from work. But at its heart, leisure is so much more. Leisure is intentional time set aside to commune with God on a natural level.

I was on retreat one summer, and in the afternoons, I would crush some trails on my mountain bike. Once back, I'd take a shower and kick my feet up for a bit. Resting there in peace and pondering on life, I said to myself, "This is leisure." It was almost like a discovery for me. *Leisure* was not a word in my vocabulary prior to that.

The essence of *going fishing* is leisure. It may be active, or it may not be. One thing, however, that leisure does not involve is digital technology—for example, the Internet, movies, and social media. Spending time in leisure is psychologically relaxing. Entertaining ourselves through digital media is mentally exhausting.

Don't get me wrong. The digital age has opened up some amazing doors. But it is not communing with God. It is being dictated to by a computer. God wants to speak to our hearts through what is *true, good,* and *beautiful.* But our brains hunger for that quick stimulus that comes through digital synapses.

One great art that has been lost in our modern culture is that of pondering, taking time to listen to our hearts. My buddy Dave used to give me a hard time because occasionally on long tow-truck runs, I'd pick up a hamburger and stop at a bridge crossing the Little Blackfoot River and ponder life. He'd shake his head. But oh, how the Lord would speak to my heart!

About the only necessary ingredient for pondering is silence. *Gunsmoke's* Matt Dillon was good at pondering. He'd be sitting on the boardwalk in front of the Dodge City jail with his feet propped up on the hitching post. Doc Adams would walk by and say, "What are you doing?" Dillon would reply, "I'm thinking."

Pondering allows our hearts to percolate. It gives space for the musings of our hearts to inform our minds. Then, through the filter of reason, we glean the good and reject the bad. To intentionally stop random cognitive discourse and listen to our hearts is to allow God to communicate with us.

Such genuine encounters with the voice of God refresh us so that we can be *fully the men and women God has created us to be*. It grounds us in sonship and renews us in mission. Pondering and leisure are at the heart of *going fishing* and are essential to being fully human.

The devil knows how good it is for man to stop and smell the roses of life. Therefore, he is happy to keep us busy. Busyness is not a virtue. It is a distraction. Most people would agree that *going fishing* is good for the soul. But many people would also say that they are too busy to do so.

If you're too busy, you're too busy. God does not want us to run around like a chicken with its head cut off. He wants us to be in constant communion with Him, which happens only if we intentionally set aside time to reconnect. God knows we live in a hectic world. Therefore, He built a day into the week for us to stop and rest in Him.

I was visiting with Grandma one day and said, "If there is one thing all of us can do to right our crazy world, it would be to bring back the Lord's Day." Since the very beginning, the Sabbath was the most sacred of all observances. After creating the world, *God rested on the seventh day.*[173] Even after the Fall, the Sabbath rest was to be strictly observed.

With the Resurrection of Jesus Christ, Christians transferred the essence of the Sabbath from Saturday to Sunday, emphasizing that Christ has triumphed over this fallen world. Thus, Sunday is now called the Lord's Day. Our Lord *came not to abolish the law, but to fulfill it.*[174] Jesus doesn't do away with the Sabbath-day principles but fulfills them into a day where we can already experience the joys of Heaven.

Jesus says in Mark's Gospel, that the "sabbath was made for man, not man for the sabbath."[175] In other words, it doesn't profit God if we take a day to stop and rest in Him. It profits us. That's why He established it. He knew that we needed a day to recharge. And He also knew that if He didn't command it, we wouldn't take it.

God said to Moses and to all of us, "Six days you shall work, but on the seventh day you shall rest; in plowing time and in harvest time you shall rest."[176] That's a tall order, especially to modern man's ears. We like to work; we like to be productive and progress. But where does the buck stop—with God or with me?

In seminary, I made a decisive move. The number of books I had to read and papers I had to write was overwhelming. The

---

[173] Genesis 2:2.
[174] Matthew 5:17.
[175] Mark 2:27.
[176] Exodus 34:21.

logical conclusion was to work on Sunday. After experiencing no reduction in stress by doing so, I decided to trust in the Lord and completely abandon schoolwork on Sundays.

The results were outstanding. The first fruit was a deep knowledge of God's providence. All of the work didn't necessarily get done, but He filled in the gaps. I learned what He wanted me to know. Through His grace, I got done what needed to get done and even got the best grades of my life.

The greater blessing that came through taking Sundays off was a proper ordering of my life. My week began to revolve around Sunday. All my efforts during the six days were ordered to resting on the seventh. Such intentionality gave a goal to strive for and a day to anticipate and look forward to.

The beauty of the Lord's Day is that it is actually the eighth day. It is the eternal day that has no beginning or end. It is the alpha and omega of the week, the source and summit of our lives. Sunday is Heaven on earth.

By centering my week on Sunday, I not only experienced peace Monday through Saturday, but I also enjoyed Sunday even more. It became not just a day to sit around and twiddle my thumbs but an authentic day of communion and recreation. If Sunday was meant for us to experience Heaven on earth, it makes sense that we would be drawn into deeper intimacy with God and one another, as well as re-created in our activity.

The Church is clear about the importance and goodness of the Lord's Day. In fact, her first precept for staying in a state of grace is to "attend Mass on Sundays and holy days of obligation and rest from servile labor."[177] The idea is to *make Sunday holy*, to

---

[177] CCC 2042.

sanctify the day and set it apart. Mass and prayer are essential to doing so. But so is rest.

Rest can get a bad rap. The heart of the Sabbath rest is to rest in God, which is not passive. God is pure act. To rest in God is to be consumed by His presence. When the Church asks us to *rest from servile labor*, she means to *rest from work and activities that would impede the sanctification of Sunday*.[178] To go fishing—through authentic leisure and pondering, even if you're active—is not servile labor. But to vainly work to get ahead of the week is.

Often it is said that "as long as I enjoy what I'm doing I can be as busy as I want on Sunday." The fallacy of this is that it's the *Lord's Day*, not *my day*. Sure, God wants us to enjoy the day. But the point of Sunday is to recenter my life on Him, not on myself.

God knows our lives can be hectic. That's why He's here to help. His day helps us put our lives in their proper perspective, which comes from being beloved sons and daughters. To truly take a Sabbath rest and hallow the Lord's Day is a sacrifice. But I guarantee it will restore purpose and mission to the world.

Cowboy Catholicism is a way of life. It's like ranching. You don't clock in and clock out. It is a 24/8 venture. The beauty of this methodology is that it brings harmony to life. Sure, there's work to be done. But when the neighbor shows up, we stop and have coffee.

We've all heard the saying of having a lot of irons in the fire, meaning that we have a lot of things going on. Such situations can be overwhelming if not handled correctly. Left unattended, certain responsibilities can get too hot while others get too cold.

The secret to juggling a lot of projects is what I call *iron rotation*. In branding, you grab the iron closest to the fire, use it, then put

---

[178] Ibid.

it back in the rear of the lineup. Then you grab the next, use it, and put it back in the rear. Eventually they all start coming back around again. Hence, some don't get too hot from not being used and others don't grow cold from getting used too much.

It's not an exact science, but when we find ourselves with *a lot on our plate*, many projects in front of us, don't get overwhelmed. Just rotate our irons. Give adequate amounts of attention to those closest to the fire, then move on to the next one. This tends to make life a bit more bite-sized and palatable.

But don't forget the *go fishing* iron. It is important to a well-balanced life as well to keeping the fire of Christ stoked in our hearts. It keeps us grounded in our sonship while reminding us that the salvation of the world does not depend on us. We each have a part to play, which is not to be taken lightly. But Jesus is our Savior. It is He who leads us back to the Father.

I love being a Catholic Cowboy. It combines my two favorite things in life: God and ranching. I've been on both sides of the fence, sometimes too churchy and other times too ranchy. But the best experience of life I've found is in the middle, with no fences. It's like having an *open-range heart*.

God wants us to be whole, fully the men and women He has created us to be. So often in my life, I've been bifurcated, trying to walk this lane and that. Life in Christ is integrating. It unites body and soul, interests and mission, Heaven and earth. Jesus incorporates us into the very life of the Trinity. The Father, the Son, and the Holy Spirit are one, *and* unique at the same time.

I've been bucked off of life more than once. But the true mark of a cowboy is not if we get bucked off or not, but whether we get back on again. The encouragement of the Holy Spirit is always here to help us saddle back up. Life is an education. We learn from the past so as not to be surprised in the future.

Once we have a seat in life, I find the best way to stay there is in the arms of our Blessed Mother, Mary. The reality of getting dumped again is real. But in her arms, I don't fear it. Evil can't reach us there. Entrusting ourselves to Mary's care is like being asleep in the boat while we sail across the chaotic waters of life.

The Catholic Cowboy Way is about having fun and getting the job done. It is normal for life on earth to be crazy. But that doesn't mean we have to get caught up in it. Jesus came *that we may have life and have it to the full.*[179] But He also said, *In this world you will have trouble.*[180]

Life is a bronc. We can either come to terms with that and enjoy the ride or sit on the sidelines and cry. I choose the former. Confidence comes from experience. We have to saddle up if we're gonna learn to ride. Getting dumped in the dirt teaches us something. So we can't be afraid to get back on again.

Fear is the greatest tactic of the devil. But he is all bark, so to speak. If we stand up to him with truth and love, he will tuck his tail and run. If we don't, though, he will scare us to death. I firmly believe that if we don't follow fear, we can experience Heaven on earth.

The greatest lesson in life I've learned is that of sonship. The more we live out of our hearts as beloved children of God the Father, the happier we will be. This sounds too good to be true. But it's not. We are sons before we're fathers, daughters before mothers.

Our Lord is Jesus Christ: Son then Messiah. His whole ministry stemmed from His relationship with the Father. Once this truth settled into my life, I found consistent peace and joy. No longer did I try to be someone else, but I trusted that the priest God wants me to be is the man He created me to be.

[179] John 10:10.
[180] John 16:33.

Lord knows I'm far from perfect. But we're all works in progress. As St. Paul says, *may God who has begun a good work in you bring it to completion.*[181] Sonship is the way to a happy and purposeful life on earth. It mirrors Heaven, where we will all dwell as sons and daughters, brothers and sisters, who serve God and one another from the gifts He has given us.

I'm not a self-made man, nor are any of us. We learn by example. The men and women whom I grew up around and the people I choose to surround myself with today continue to teach me how to live and how to love. We are products of our environment, both past and present.

I am who I am because Dad loved Mom. Love is caught more than taught. The more we see love, the more we are able to imitate it. It is not enough just to know about the Father's love for us; we have to experience it. Fortunately, it is everywhere. All we really need to do is open our hearts in true Christian faith.

Jesus is the greatest role model a man can have. He not only leads us back to the Father; He also teaches how to live life. He's not just a historical figure but also a Man who continues to guide us through the Holy Spirit dwelling in our hearts. To follow the Lord with all our heart, all our soul, all our mind, and all our strength is the Catholic Cowboy Way.

[181] Philippians 1:6.

About the Author

Fr. Bryce Lungren was blessed to grow up in a family with deep Wyoming roots. After graduating high school in Worland, Wyoming, in 1998, he moved to Montana, where he worked in the world and grew in his Catholic Faith. In 2008, he entered the seminary. He earned a bachelor of arts in philosophy at Mount Angel Seminary in St. Benedict, Oregon, followed by a master of divinity and a bachelor of sacred theology at St. John Vianney Theological Seminary in Denver, Colorado. He was ordained a priest for the Diocese of Cheyenne on the feast of the Sacred Heart of Jesus in 2018 and is currently the associate pastor of St. Matthew's Catholic Church and surrounding missions in Gillette, Wyoming.

Sophia Institute

Sophia Institute is a nonprofit institution that seeks to nurture the spiritual, moral, and cultural life of souls and to spread the gospel of Christ in conformity with the authentic teachings of the Roman Catholic Church.

Sophia Institute Press fulfills this mission by offering translations, reprints, and new publications that afford readers a rich source of the enduring wisdom of mankind.

Sophia Institute also operates the popular online resource CatholicExchange.com. *Catholic Exchange* provides world news from a Catholic perspective as well as daily devotionals and articles that will help readers to grow in holiness and live a life consistent with the teachings of the Church.

In 2013, Sophia Institute launched Sophia Institute for Teachers to renew and rebuild Catholic culture through service to Catholic education. With the goal of nurturing the spiritual, moral, and cultural life of souls, and an abiding respect for the role and work of teachers, we strive to provide materials and programs that are at once enlightening to the mind and ennobling to the heart; faithful and complete, as well as useful and practical.

Sophia Institute gratefully recognizes the Solidarity Association for preserving and encouraging the growth of our apostolate over the course of many years. Without their generous and timely support, this book would not be in your hands.

www.SophiaInstitute.com
www.CatholicExchange.com
www.SophiaInstituteforTeachers.org

Sophia Institute Press® is a registered trademark of Sophia Institute.
Sophia Institute is a tax-exempt institution as defined by the
Internal Revenue Code, Section 501(c)(3). Tax ID 22-2548708.